DOING CHURCH

DOING CHURCH

A BIBLICAL GUIDE FOR LEADING MINISTRIES THROUGH CHANGE

AUBREY MALPHURS

kregel
PUBLICATIONS

Grand Rapids, MI 49501

Doing Church: A Biblical Guide for Leading Ministries Through Change

© 1999 by Aubrey Malphurs

Published by Kregel Publications, a division of Kregel, Inc., P.O. Box 2607, Grand Rapids, MI 49501. Kregel Publications provides trusted, biblical publications for Christian growth and service. Your comments and suggestions are valued.

For more information about Kregel Publications, visit our web site: www.kregel.com

Cover design: Nicholas G. Richardson
Book design: Kevin Ingram

Library of Congress Cataloging-in-Publication Data
Malphurs, Aubrey.
   Doing church: a biblical buide for leading ministries through change / by Aubrey Malphurs.
      p.   cm.
   Includes bibliographical references.
   1. Pastoral theology—Biblical teaching. 2. Church—Biblical teaching. 3. Bible. N.T.—Hermeneutics. I. Title.
BS2545.P45M25   1999   253—dc21   99-36575
                                                                      CIP
ISBN 0-8254-3187-5

Printed in the United States of America

1 2 3 4 5 / 03 02 01 00 99

Contents

Introduction

Beginning with the cultural revolution of the 1960s, gale-like winds of change have swept over North American society in general and the church in particular, uprooting everything in their path. How have these forces affected the followers of Christ?

The Desperate Situation

Presently, the church isn't doing well. I suspect that if the typical congregation were to check into the hospital, the physicians would place its members on life support. Perhaps as many as 80 to 85 percent of believers find themselves either resting on a spiritual plateau or facing steep decline. At the same time, 60 to 80 percent of the entire population remains unchurched. How has the church responded to these dire conditions?

Congregations across North America—and especially in the United States—have jettisoned long-held models (or paradigms) of church ministry for newer ones. (I call these *new paradigm* churches.) For instance, church leaders have replaced religious traditions that began in Europe with ones that originated in America. And there has been the rise of the megachurch movement. This has resulted in the proliferation of more *large* churches than ever before in the history of the United States.

The Concern

The rise of new paradigm churches and the megachurch movement has caused a great deal of concern among Christian leaders. They're asking, "Where are all these changes taking us? Is the church dangerously perched on some slippery ecclesiological slope and about to slide into heresy?"

Some Christian leaders would answer *no* to these questions. These leaders can be divided into two groups. The first are the church pragmatists. They would point to the success of many of the new paradigm churches in accomplishing the Great Commission (Matt. 28:19–20). In fact, they note that many churches "made in America" (so to speak) are thriving, while those "made in Europe" are doing poorly. Supposedly the success of the new paradigm church is proof of its legitimacy and the Lord's blessing on it. If one were to ask the leaders of these congregations to explain the biblical basis for the way they conduct their ministry, they wouldn't be able to do so. All they could do is say, "It's working!"

The second group is made up of the new paradigm leaders. They see the inadequacy of the church remaining isolated, refusing to respond to changes in society, and clinging to outdated traditions inherited from Europe. They also recognize the need for change and are willing to take some risks in order to make adjustments. Though these Christian leaders want to be true to the Bible, they aren't sure how far the church should go in changing. In their quieter moments, they wonder whether they're on the slippery slope mentioned above. Despite their concerns, they would prefer to launch out in a new direction rather than be stuck in the past.

Other Christian leaders would answer *yes* to the slippery slope question. These leaders can be divided into two groups. The first are the church traditionalists who think that the changes taking place aren't good. Their motto is this: "If it ain't broke, don't fix it; and if it's broke, then work harder at making it work!" They're not sure what the Bible specifically says about the new paradigm churches and their unconventional approach to doing ministry, but these leaders are convinced that the Bible is against such change. They assume that much of what the church has traditionally done can be found somewhere in the Bible. "After all," they ask, "isn't that where we got these practices in the first place?" Supposedly if established traditions were good enough in the past, they should still be good today. They conclude that because all this change is harmful, it must be resisted at all costs.

The second group is the church reactionists. They're convinced that the new paradigm churches and the megachurch movement have already fallen off the slippery slope. The reactionists think the church is in a state of crisis and heading for disaster. They argue that unconventional church leaders have allowed slick marketing and pop psychology, rather than Scripture, to dictate how they should run their ministry. The reactionists claim that the pragmatists and new paradigm people have de-emphasized the difficult aspects of Christian theology. Instead of preaching sin and salvation, they're supposedly opting instead to proclaim a message of personal fulfillment.

In sympathy with the reactionists, I'm convinced that we need believers who challenge us to think theologically! The alternative is doctrinal gullibility and practical naiveté. There are some reactionists who speak out in a spirit of love and concern for all God's people, regardless of where they stand on these issues. May their tribe increase. But there are other reactionists who are uncharitable in speaking their mind. They use inflammatory language, especially as they accuse the new paradigm churches of seeking to "*entertain* the lost, *amuse* the brethren, or *cater* to the felt needs of those in attendance."[1] Such rhetoric is counterproductive, for it serves only to divide the church further.

The Critical Questions

The changes noted above and the various ways Christian leaders have responded to them give rise to a primary question: How should the church conduct its ministry? This question, in turn, leads to several subsidiary questions:

1. What does the Bible teach about the ministries of the church?
2. What is permissible and what impermissible, and how can we make a determination?
3. Does the early church provide a guide for the practices and patterns permitted in our congregations today? If so, what are they and how should they be followed?

4. What role should changes in society have on the church? How much freedom does the church have in designing its own ministries and pursuing new directions for outreach and growth? What can or must change, and what must never change in the way the church does things?

The Answer

The answer to the primary question is simple. The church should conduct its ministry according to the teaching of Scripture. This statement also holds true for the subsidiary questions. The ultimate determining factor is what the Bible says about each and every issue confronting the church.

Of course, analyzing change and responding to it in a scriptural way is rarely simple and never easy. One reason is that evangelicals interpret the Bible in different ways. This causes them to take discordant views about the teaching of Scripture concerning the ministry of the church. For example, differences of opinion exist over church polity, the mode of baptism, the different styles of worship, the role of women in the church, the presence and operation of certain spiritual gifts, the frequency of observing the Lord's Supper, when the church should meet, how the church should worship, and who should lead the service.

Differing church traditions and approaches to hermeneutics further complicate the problem.[2] Both issues exert a strong influence on how one applies the teaching of Scripture to the ministries of the church. In light of these tensions, I will discuss the different views of church ministry and a proper hermeneutic for church ministry.

The Purpose and Scope of This Book

If you're a student of the Bible, a pastor, or a leader of any kind in the church, then this book is for *you!* It will help you to conduct your ministry according to the timeless principles of the Bible.

I'm convinced that hermeneutics provides guidelines to the ministry issues you face. As your congregation moves into the twenty-first century, you need to know what it should and should not do. The answer ultimately lies in how you interpret the Bible. This book will teach you how to handle Scripture properly and to discover the biblical way for conducting church ministry.

Let's take a moment to look at the table of contents. You'll notice that I've divided the book into two parts. Part 1 addresses the problem of why many churches view ministry differently. The answer is found in how they interpret and apply the Bible, and the reason why they interpret it differently is explained in chapters 1 and 2. Chapter 1 shows how the church's traditions influence its understanding of the Bible. Chapter 2 presents the need of the church for a consistent hermeneutic, that is, a uniform way of interpreting and applying Scripture to its various ministries.

Part 2 provides a solution to the interpretation problem by presenting a clear and sound hermeneutic for the ministry. I have divided part 2 into two sections. In the first section, you'll learn some general principles for interpreting the Bible that also affect how your church does ministry. Chapter 3 of this section introduces the principle of authorial intent. You'll learn that the only way to understand what the Bible says is by determining what its human authors meant in their writings. For example, you'll see how this concept is crucial for interpreting Acts properly, which some have called the church history book of the New Testament. Chapter 4 emphasizes the importance of knowing and recognizing different biblical genres (namely, literary styles). For instance, you'll see how knowledge of the genre of Acts (which is historical narrative) affects the proper interpretation and application of passages relating to the ministry and growth of the church.

The second section of part 2 consists of four chapters that present some specific principles for interpreting passages of Scripture concerned with the ministry of the church. Each chapter poses a question and then answers that question using principles of hermeneutics.

Chapter 5 covers the negative versus the positive hermeneutic. It asks the question, "Must we find our church practices in the Bible?" Chapter 6 presents the descriptive versus the prescriptive hermeneutic. It asks the question, "Must the church follow the descriptive ministry practices in the Bible as well as those man-dated in Scripture?" Chapter 7 covers the hermeneutic of patterns versus principles. It asks the question, "Must the church today fol-low the ministry patterns of the apostolic church as well as its principles?" Finally, chapter 8 presents the hermeneutic of func-tions versus forms. It asks the question, "What role should changes in society have on the way the church conducts its ministries?"

At the end of each chapter I've provided questions. Their pur-pose is to help you think through and apply the material in a chap-ter. In order for you to get the most out of this book, I strongly recommend that you work through the questions. In fact, you might consider both reading the book and answering the questions with the leadership team of your church. Doing this will allow all of you to be on the same hermeneutical page, especially as you wrestle with how your church "does ministry."

Endnotes

1. John F. MacArthur Jr., "How Shall We Then Worship?" in *The Com-ing Evangelical Crisis* (Chicago, Ill.: Moody, 1996), 185.
2. Hermeneutics is the science of understanding what the Bible says.

PART 1

THE PROBLEM–
DIFFERENT VIEWS
OF CHURCH MINISTRY

The different views that various denominations and congregations have regarding how churches should conduct their ministries are ✓ based on different interpretations of the Bible. This raises several important questions. Why are there so many different interpretations? Why can't all churches agree on what the Bible says about ministry and simply get on with the tasks? What does the Bible teach directly or implicitly, and what doesn't it teach about the ministry of the church?

There are two reasons for the different views of church ministry. One has to do with the influence of tradition in the church, and this is the topic of study in chapter 1. The second reason has to do with the hermeneutic (or lack of one) adopted by the church, and this is the topic of study in chapter 2.

1

The Influence of Tradition in the Church

In this chapter we are investigating the question, "Why do so many churches interpret the Bible so differently?" One reason is the presence of widely divergent traditions. I define church traditions as the nonbiblical[1] customs, practices, and ideas that church people attempt to observe, preserve, and pass on to the next generation. They serve to preserve the past. These traditions include such practices as a Wednesday night prayer meeting, singing the great hymns of the faith, maintaining a Sunday school program, the way in which a church takes the offering, and so forth.

Traditions are nonbiblical because Scripture doesn't mandate them. The church observes these practices in such a way that in time they become an integral part of the congregation's overall identity and ministry. Because the church so highly values these customs, they attempt to preserve and pass them on to the next generation. As one deacon said, "After all, if they're good enough for us, they should be good enough for our kids and grandkids!"

As long as the church exists, it will embrace numerous traditions. And it's these traditions—both good and bad—that exert a profound influence on how each congregation views and interprets the Bible. Traditions act as a modern-day lens through which believers filter what they read from the ancient writings of Scripture. In this chapter, I want to focus attention on two major categories of tradition: church tradition and personal tradition.

Church, or Denominational, Tradition

The first major category of tradition is church, or denominational, tradition. Rex Koivisto suggests that two kinds of this tradition exist: interpretive tradition and external tradition.[2]

Interpretive Tradition

Interpretive tradition consists of those customs that we assert are the *clear* teaching of the Bible. Koivisto writes, "Interpretive tradition claims to be based on the interpretation of the Bible."[3] The danger with this type of tradition is brought to light in the definition. We're convinced that these aren't customs but rather the teaching of Scripture. We don't recognize them as tradition, or we don't recognize the possibility that they might be tradition. Instead, we think that the Bible mandates these practices, and thus we consider them binding on all believers.

How can we distinguish between the clear teaching of Scripture and our interpretive traditions? The solution is to determine what we believe are the essentials and nonessentials of the faith. At issue is what we and other evangelicals would put under each category. If the majority of orthodox believers put what you believe under the nonessentials of the faith, then you may be dealing with interpretative tradition. While I understand that the majority isn't always correct, we should at least be willing to consider this possibility when faced with such a situation.

The Essentials of the Faith

The essentials of the faith are those propositional truths that not only are clearly taught in the Bible but also are necessary for one to hold in order to be considered orthodox. These essentials are considered to be the central tenets of the evangelical belief system. Because they're at the heart of the gospel, there's no room for disagreement. Should people reject one or more of these views, their version of Christianity may not be orthodox. As you can see, this isn't interpretive tradition.

What are the essentials of the faith? Let's look at five that are worth mentioning. First is the inspiration and inerrancy of the Bible as the Word of God. Second is the existence of only one true God as three coequal and coeternal persons (namely, the Trinity). Third is the deity and substitutionary atonement of Christ, which includes the concept of salvation by faith apart from human works. Fourth is the bodily resurrection of Christ. And fifth is Jesus' physical return to earth.

> **The Essentials of the Faith**
> 1. The inspiration and inerrancy of the Bible as the Word of God
> 2. The existence of only one true God as three coequal and coeternal persons (namely, the Trinity)
> 3. The deity and substitutionary atonement of Christ
> 4. The bodily resurrection of Christ
> 5. The physical return of Christ

In light of these essentials of the faith, what should our response be to others? We should pursue unity and love with those who agree with us on these points of doctrine. We must agree on the essentials, or we can't minister together in any way.

This is a relational, not an organizational, unity based on a common orthodox faith (John 17:20–23; Eph. 4:3). Christ commands that we also love one another as fellow disciples (John 13:34–35; 15:12–14). We're willing to relate to one another in various ways, including citywide evangelistic crusades, theological societies, and other ecclesiastical endeavors.

These essentials are both inclusive and exclusive. They include people of like mind, but they exclude people who don't agree with us on key points of doctrine. Examples of the latter would be those of a theologically liberal persuasion, Mormons, Jehovah's Witnesses, and Unitarians.

The Nonessentials of the Faith

The nonessentials of the faith are views we hold that are based on Scripture, tradition, or both. This would be an example of interpretive tradition. The nonessentials aren't as clear biblically, and that's why evangelicals disagree over them. One group's essentials of the faith may be another's nonessentials. Though a doctrine may be "nonessential," the church holding it believes it is correct and strongly supported in Scripture. Choosing to agree or disagree on these finer points of doctrine doesn't affect one's salvation or standing before Christ (as would holding to the essentials of the faith).

The following are some examples that have proven to be nonessential teachings of Scripture that may affect the organization and ministries of a church. The first item is church government. Most churches have adopted either an Episcopal, Presbyterian, or Congregational style. A second item is the mode of baptism. Most who baptize practice either immersion, sprinkling, or pouring. A third item is the efficacy of the Lord's Supper. The key question is this: Do the elements convey grace to the recipients? The positions range from an emphatic *yes* to an equally emphatic *no*.

A fourth nonessential item is the role of women in the church. The positions range from full participation (including ordination) to no participation at all. A fifth item concerns spiritual gifts. The positions range from all the gifts are for today, to only some of the gifts are present and operative. A sixth item concerns when the church meets. Some argue that it must be on the first day of the week, while others insist that any day is permissible. The seventh item concerns what the church does when it meets. For instance, some argue that the congregation must serve communion every time it meets, while others think that this isn't necessary.

Some Nonessentials of the Faith
1. The form of church government
2. The mode of baptism
3. The efficacy of the Lord's Supper
4. The role of women in the church

5. The presence and permanency of certain spiritual gifts
6. The time and place when the church meets
7. The ministries performed by the church when it meets

What should our response be to others regarding the nonessentials of the faith? Scripture teaches that we're to pursue liberty and love. Liberty involves the realization that it's okay to take a firm position on these issues. Nevertheless, it's important to recognize that we're in the realm of interpretive tradition. Though we think Scripture best supports our view, other godly evangelicals can legitimately hold differing opinions for what seem to be good reasons. Despite these differences each group is still orthodox.

Christian liberty says that we must be willing to grant others these distinctions and still love them and hold them in high regard. Preserving the "unity of the faith" (Eph. 4:13) means treating others who differ with us on the nonessentials with kindness and compassion (John 13:34–35; 15:12–14, 17). We refuse to judge and malign them (Rom. 14:9–13). We also recoil at the idea of claiming that we're "the remnant," namely, the only ones with the truth, while all other Christian groups are wrong and condemned. Instead, we choose to treat one another as fellow believers in Christ.

In summary, consider the following familiar statement: In the essentials, unity; in the nonessentials, liberty; and in all things (both the essentials and nonessentials), love. The concepts of the essentials and nonessentials raise several applicational questions for the church.

1. Where do we draw lines of doctrinal distinction, if at all?
2. Do we let our views on the nonessentials of the faith separate us? If so, how much, or to what extent?[4]
3. Can we do anything together at all? If so, what is it and to what extent? (Perhaps we can meet together in a fellowship or cooperate in some joint ministry ventures.)

Here's another key question: Are nonessentials important enough that we want to do any of the following?

1. Deny someone membership in the church
2. Keep someone off a church board
3. Include nonessentials in a doctrinal statement
4. Exclude someone from speaking or teaching at church
5. Divide or split a church
6. Form a new denomination or ministry organization

External Tradition

Another kind of church tradition is what Koivisto calls external tradition. This ecclesiastical practice makes no claim to be based on Scripture. However, some in our churches may wrongly assume—whether consciously or unconsciously—that some or all external tradition is scriptural. They may justify their views with this line of reasoning: "We've always done it this way. Therefore it must be based on the Bible!"

> **Two Types of Church Tradition**
> 1. Interpretive tradition—Based on the Bible?
> 2. External tradition—Not based on the Bible?

Some examples of external tradition include the following: the form of Christian liturgy; the type of church building; the presence and use of pews, kneelers, a communion table, an altar, a baptistry, stained glass windows, collection plates, and carillon;[5] the wearing of crucifixes, clerical robes, and collars; and the holding of Sunday school.

The applicational problem with external tradition is the adoption of customs that are harmful to the life of the church. According to my definition, tradition isn't based on Scripture. Therefore, good tradition represents the church's practices that it thinks are subservient to the teaching of the Bible (figure 1). This means that bad tradition represents the church's customs that it thinks are *equal to or above* the teaching of the Bible (figure 2). Those embracing bad tradition insist that it is binding on all Christians either because "we've always done it that way," or because it's our preference, or because we're afraid to change.

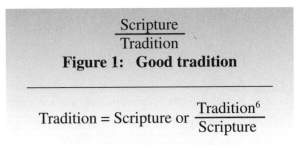

$$\frac{\text{Scripture}}{\text{Tradition}}$$

Figure 1:   Good tradition

$$\text{Tradition} = \text{Scripture or } \frac{\text{Tradition}^6}{\text{Scripture}}$$

Figure 2:   Bad tradition

Personal Tradition

Personal tradition is a second major category that affects the church's interpretation of the Bible.[7] As modern-day believers, we bring our own personal traditions to the study of the inspired text. However, the people who wrote the Bible lived in a different world and held different traditions, even among themselves. Since our world is vastly different from theirs, our personal traditions may not be the same as theirs. This affects how we interpret the Bible in general and how we conduct ministry in particular.

What makes up our personal traditions? These consist of the experiences we've accumulated while growing up in our particular culture. Of personal importance are the customs we've adopted from our experiences with our faith and the different churches we've attended.

These traditions affect how we view both the Old and New Testaments. Our tendency is to read our cultural ideas into Scripture. A good example of this is the famous painting entitled *The Last Supper* by Leonardo da Vinci (1452–1519). He lived in a culture where people customarily sat on chairs while dining around a table. That's why he painted Jesus and His disciples doing the same thing when they ate a final meal on the evening preceding His crucifixion. However, the custom in Bible times was for people to recline on the left side of a low platform. While they rested on their left elbow, they would eat with their right hand, and they would have their feet extended outward (see John 13:23).

Most likely, if we grew up in a church where new converts were immersed in a baptistry located up in front of the sanctuary, that is what we envision when we read about baptism in Scripture. The same tendency exists when we partake of communion, preach the Word, evangelize the lost, and conduct worship services. Our religious traditions color our interpretation of the biblical text. As one old timer put it, "If the organ and piano were good enough for Jesus and Paul, they should be good enough for us!"

This cultural bias presents two difficulties. First, we unconsciously assume that everyone today (as well as in the Bible times) shares our traditions and interprets Scripture as we do. In such a situation, we not only miss what God's Word is teaching but also fail to understand the viewpoint of others and communicate with them in ways they can grasp.

The second difficulty is that our traditions prevent us from understanding and applying Scripture. For example, imagine growing up in a church where the tradition is for the pastor to do all the work of the ministry. We're preconditioned to think that's the way a church should operate. This, in turn, skews our understanding of a passage such as Ephesians 4:11–13. In these verses, Paul taught that gifted members as well as leaders are responsible for the equipping of the saints. They then do the work of the ministry so that the body of Christ might be spiritually strengthened. In other words, Paul was not just writing to pastors, but also to all believers.

Two Categories of Tradition
1. Church, or denominational, tradition
2. Personal tradition

Questions for Reflection and Discussion

1. What are some of your church, or denominational, traditions? Which ones are interpretive traditions? Which are external traditions?

2. What do you believe are the core essentials of the faith? What are the nonessentials?

3. Where would you draw the line in the area of the nonessentials? What action would you take over these differences?

4. Are you willing to discuss your differences over the nonessentials with those who differ from you? Why or why not? Is it possible for you to listen carefully to what they say without being defensive? If the answer is *no*, why not?

5. How difficult would it be for you to modify what you believe about the nonessentials of the faith? Would you be willing to change your views, especially if it meant differing with your church or denomination? Why or why not? If necessary, would you take a public stand on these differences? Why or why not?

6. Identify some of your own personal traditions. How might they affect the way you interpret Scripture?

Endnotes

1. By nonbiblical, I don't mean *un*biblical. In other words, these traditions don't necessarily contradict Scripture although some might (Mark 7: 8–9).
2. Rex A. Koivisto, *One Lord, One Faith* (Wheaton: Victor, 1993), 145.
3. Ibid.
4. In answer to this question, some have embraced second-degree separation as well as first-degree separation. First-degree separation is when Christians separate from others who differ with them over some issue. It is usually nonessential to the faith. Second-degree separation is when Christians separate from other believers who agree with them but who refuse to practice first-degree separation.
5. Carillon are tuned bells sounded by hammers, which are controlled from a keyboard.
6. In this scheme of thinking, tradition equals Scripture.

7. Gordan Fee also observes this aspect of tradition. He calls it a "non-technical nuance to tradition, which refers to that entire set of experiences and settings making up one's personal history, that one brings to the biblical text before ever a page is opened" (Gordon D. Fee, *Gospel and Spirit* [Peabody, Mass.: Hendrickson, 1991], 68).

2

The Need of a Hermeneutic for the Church

In chapter 1, I explained that tradition is one reason for all the different interpretations of how the church should conduct its ministry. The differing approaches to hermeneutics is a second reason. The key question is this: "How do we interpret the Bible?" Hermeneutics answers by providing various principles for understanding and applying Scripture. A knowledge of these principles and their skillful application will result in a more accurate interpretation of God's Word.

People who attend and lead churches have some sort of hermeneutic for interpreting the Bible. Most often, it's the same literal approach they use when reading a newspaper, magazine article, or good novel. Is this a good hermeneutic? To a limited extent the answer is *yes*. The problem is that reading and understanding the morning paper and a book of Scripture such as Acts involves differing levels of complexity.

For the most part, we understand the words, figurative language, and type of literature (or genre) found in a newspaper. Acts also uses words and figurative language in the context of a particular literary type. However, Luke wrote it in the first century, not the twenty-first century. This chronological and cultural gap has led to numerous interpretive differences and even theological heresy among some religious groups.

This example underscores the twofold need of the church in

the area of hermeneutics. First, believers need a general, overall knowledge of hermeneutics. That is the topic of the first section of this chapter. Second, Christians need a specific and consistent hermeneutic for interpreting the Bible, especially as it relates to church matters such as organization and ministries. That is the topic of the second section of this chapter.

The Need for a General Knowledge of Hermeneutics

Believers need a general knowledge of hermeneutics so that they can properly interpret the Bible. This is because the books of Scripture were penned over a period of about fifteen hundred years. The human authors wrote in different ancient languages (Hebrew, Aramaic, and Greek), came from different cultures, and lived during different times in history. In order for us to understand the Bible's general message and the specific passages that relate to the church, we need to consider these three factors. Hermeneutics has articulated general principles to help us better understand what the Bible is saying. In the following discussion, we will discover that we need to interpret Scripture literally and that we need to take into consideration the historic, cultural, and linguistic gaps.

A Literal Interpretation

A key principle of interpretation is to take what the Bible says in its literal sense. Tragically, liberals and conservatives alike have misunderstood this concept. They claim that a literal hermeneutic fails to recognize that various writers of Scripture in certain situations used figurative language to communicate their message. Their assertion, of course, is incorrect.

So what does it mean to interpret the Bible literally? The idea is to understand Scripture in a "normal," "common sense," or "ordinary" way. We take what the authors say in a literal way or at "face value" unless they give obvious clues that we should understand their words in some other way. For example, a crassly literal approach would be out of place when the writer has used figurative language. But even in this situation, we interpret different forms of expression (such as similes and metaphors) to discover the message the author wanted to convey. We ask, "Why did the writer use a figure of speech?" and "What idea was he seeking to communicate by using this form of expression?"

For example, John 1:29 says, "Look, the Lamb of God, who takes away the sin of the world!"[1] If we interpret this passage literally, we would conclude that Jesus is a four-footed mammal being raised for its flesh and wool. Clearly this would be an absurdity! But if we recognized that John the Baptist was using a figure of speech, the problem disappears. By taking into account the language, history, and culture of the day, we learn that in the Old Testament the Israelites sacrificed lambs at the Passover feast and as offerings (Exod. 12:21; Lev. 14:10–25). John the Baptist was saying that Jesus is the offering whom God would give as a sacrifice for the sins of the world (Isa. 52:13–53:12).

The use of literal and figurative language also affects how we understand and apply some early-church practices. For example, in Acts 20:7, Luke wrote that Paul and his companions joined other believers in Troas[2] to "break bread." The issue here is whether "breaking bread" refers to a fellowship meal or is a figure or technical term for the Lord's Supper. Most exegetes conclude the latter.

The Historical, Linguistic, and Cultural Gaps

When we interpret the Bible, we must take into account the historical, linguistic, and cultural gaps between ancient times and today. Let's briefly examine each of these areas.

The Historical Gap

God has spoken to humankind within the context of time. A basic knowledge of that context is vital for understanding the Bible. For example, some argue that Christians today must slavishly imitate the customs and practices of the early church. Tragically, these folks overlook the fact that the historical context of the early church is vastly different from the world in which we live. For instance, the New Testament had not been completely written, there were apostles and prophets, and miracles were being performed. None of these things are true today. That's why we need to ask whether the believers must mimic the routines of the early church.

The Linguistic Gap

The human authors of Scripture didn't speak and write in English. Rather, their native tongues were Hebrew, Aramaic, and Greek. Consider Paul. He was a Jew who knew these three ancient languages. While the Old Testament was written in Hebrew and Aramaic, the apostles' letters (as well as the rest of the New Testament) were written in Greek. In order to interpret the Bible with the highest proficiency, it is necessary to consider the original languages in which Scripture was written.

I sense today that a subtle shift away from a knowledge of the original languages is taking place among seminary-trained pastors who have embraced a new paradigm approach to ministry. Perhaps this is because they have thrown the proverbial "baby out with the bath water." Finding that they've graduated from seminary generally unprepared to lead a church, they "write off" their graduate religious training in the original languages as being irrelevant and useless.[3] I would encourage these ministers to value and use their knowledge of Hebrew, Aramaic, and Greek, along with the leadership training they received.[4]

The Cultural Gap

The writers of Scripture lived in a culture that is vastly different from our own. The customs, beliefs, and social forms of their day affected the way they formulated their ideas and penned their thoughts. Incidentally, there are many different cultures represented in the pages of Scripture (such as Hebrew, Egyptian, Assyrian, Babylonian, Greek, and Roman). The Roman, Greek, and Hebrew cultures had a pronounced influence on the New Testament. For instance, we see this influence in Acts, where cultures often collided as the gospel crossed social as well as geographical boundaries.

Let's spend a few moments considering Acts 6:1–7. As the early church grew, increasing numbers of Grecian Jews began to join the faith. Though they were of Jewish descent, they spoke

Greek, were raised in a Hellenistic culture, and used the Greek translation of the Old Testament (the Septuagint). In contrast, the Hebraic Jews spoke Aramaic, were raised in Palestine, and used the Hebrew Old Testament. It's no wonder that, given these vast differences, tension would arise in the early church. In this case the Grecian Jews asserted that their widows were being discriminated against in the daily distribution of food. Rather than ignore the problem, the apostles sought a solution that would be equitable and culturally sensitive. The seven believers who were chosen to oversee the administrative task of food distribution evidently were Hellenists, for all their names were Greek.

Another example is found in Acts 15. As increasing numbers of Gentiles became Christians, a dispute arose over whether they had to observe the Mosaic law, including the rite of circumcision, in order to be saved. The leaders of the Jerusalem Council determined that the answer was *no*. But they did ask Gentile believers to abstain from certain foods so that they would not offend their fellow Jews in the faith (vv. 19–21).

Much more could be said about general principles of hermeneutics. In fact, there are several good books on this subject worth considering.[5] In addition to what I've said here, I will devote more attention to the subject in chapters 3 and 4.[6]

Two General Hermeneutical Principles

1. We should interpret the Bible literally, unless there is a strong indication in the text to do otherwise (for example, the presence of figurative language).
2. When we interpret the Bible, we should take into account the historical, linguistic, and cultural gaps between ancient times and today.

The Need of a Specific Hermeneutic for Church Matters

Believers not only need a general knowledge of hermeneutics (as important as it is) but also an understanding of how a specific hermeneutic can be applied to Christian work. We want to discuss some key hermeneutical principles for interpreting and applying the Bible in the way we "do church." This would be an approach to biblical interpretation that gives guidelines on how to use Scripture properly to conduct ministry in the church.

The Bible has much to say on this matter, especially in the New Testament. Of particular interest to our discussion are the book of Acts and the letters of Paul. Here is the key hermeneutical question facing many pastors and other church leaders: "How do we interpret these texts for the church? For example, should congregations today emulate the practices of the early church?"

Tragically, while all in ministry have to wrestle with these issues to some degree, few have addressed them in depth. The few who have (much to their credit) are the following: the Brethren, the Restorationists, and a few believers such as New Testament scholar Gordon Fee.

The Brethren

The Brethren (also known to some as the Plymouth Brethren and the Christian Brethren) are a free evangelical Protestant group. This group began as a reactionary movement to certain sectarian attitudes that were dividing the churches in Ireland and England in the 1820s and 1830s. Today the Brethren are divided into the Open Brethren and the Exclusive Brethren.

The Brethren argue that Scripture not only provides theological truth on what the church should believe but also practical truth on how congregations should conduct their ministry. The Brethren tend to congregate around ecclesiological issues and believe that they have recovered the teaching of the early church on how all congregations should do the work of the Lord. They take seriously the practices of the early church and look to the New Testament for direction on how to conduct their meetings. Thus, the Brethren have developed a hermeneutic for church ministry. You will find their views expressed in numerous tracts and booklets.

The Restorationists

The Restorationists are a religious group that began in the nineteenth century on the American frontier. They consist of the Christian Church (or Disciples of Christ) and the Churches of Christ. They have been influenced in their thinking by the views of such religious leaders as James O'Kelly in Virginia, Abner Jones and Elias Smith in New England, Barton Stone in Kentucky, and Thomas and Alexander Campbell in West Virginia. These men represent four different movements that eventually merged together into one group with a common purpose and agenda.

The Restorationists attempt to follow the Bible closely in the areas of ecclesiology. Like the Brethren, they have developed a hermeneutic for directing the ministry of the church. This is reflected in their statement that "where the Bible speaks, they speak, and where the Bible is silent, they are silent." In effect, the Restorationists are arguing that the church should do only what is found in the Bible. Their hermeneutic says that congregational practices should be patterned after those of the early church.

Gordon Fee

In a book entitled *Gospel and Spirit*, Gordon Fee focuses on a hermeneutic for church. The book is helpful, for it wrestles with the hermeneutics of the New Testament. Chapters 6 and 9 are especially useful, for in them the author deals with how heremeneutics affects the way in which the church conducts its ministry.

Chapter 6 deals with hermeneutics and historical precedent. Here Fee asks whether the historical and descriptive experience of the early church in Acts is normative for today's congregations. Chapter 9 deals with some exegetical and hermeneutical observations on church order and whether all churches are to replicate and practice the way the early church organized itself and went about its business. In effect, Fee examines the hermeneutical principles of the Brethren, the Restorationists, and similar religious groups.

It's commendable that these religious groups have tried to address the issue to some degree. Yet all but Fee seem inconsistent in their observations and conclusions and in the application of their hermeneutic. We will see some examples of this inconsistency in chapters 5 through 8.

Good material is available on general hermeneutics. However, little is available for interpreting specific passages on church ministry. Consequently, one purpose of this book is to provide a consistent hermeneutic that guides the church in conducting its ministries both now and in the future.

Questions for Reflection and Discussion

1. What is your understanding of literal interpretation? Do you interpret the Bible literally? Why or why not?

2. When you interpret the Bible, do you consider the historical, linguistic, and cultural gaps between people in ancient times and people living today? Why or why not? What difference might this knowledge make in your interpretation of the Scriptures?

3. As a pastor or church leader, have you had any training in hermeneutics? If the answer is *yes*, what kind was it? If you haven't had any training in hermeneutics, what might you do to enhance your interpretive skills?

4. Are you familiar with the teachings and views of either the Brethren churches or the Restorationists? If *yes*, what are the specific doctrines? How much do you actually know about them? Has the teaching of either of these groups had any influence on you? If *yes*, in what way and to what extent?

Endnotes

1. Unless otherwise noted, all Scripture quotations are taken from the New International Version.
2. Troas was an important city on the coast of Mysia in northwest Asia Minor (modern Turkey).
3. The problem is that most evangelical seminaries focus their attention on preparing future pastors to perform for one hour on Sunday morning. When these students graduate and go out into the world, they quickly discover that regardless of how important it is to preach

and teach God's Word, the battle is often won or lost in their skills and abilities to lead the church throughout the rest of the week.

4. Far too many seminaries spend little time helping future pastors develop their leadership skills and abilities, which are so vital to ministry in today's world. I would suggest that those students who find themselves in this situation spend their time at seminary in an internship with a pastor who exhibits leadership skills and abilities.

5. I would suggest that you begin with the following: Gordon D. Fee and Douglas Stuart, *How to Read the Bible for All It's Worth* (Grand Rapids: Zondervan, 1981); and Roy B. Zuck, *Basic Bible Interpretation* (Wheaton: Victor, 1991). An excellent book on the application of Scripture is written by Jack Kuhatschek, *Applying the Bible* (Grand Rapids: Zondervan, 1990).

6. Chapter 3 introduces the principle of authorial intent, while chapter 4 emphasizes the importance of knowing and recognizing different biblical genres (namely, literary styles).

PART 2

THE SOLUTION–
A HERMENEUTIC FOR
CHURCH MINISTRY

Part 1 answered the following questions: Why are there so many different interpretations? Why can't all churches agree on what the Bible says about ministry and simply get on with the tasks? What does the Bible teach directly or implicitly, and what doesn't it teach about the ministry of the church? The answers relate to how different church groups interpret and apply the Bible.

In chapter 1, we discovered that the traditions of a denomination or congregation strongly affect how it understands Scripture. In chapter 2, we found that the church lacks a specific, consistent hermeneutic for interpreting Scripture. There is a need for an interpretive approach that relates to the particular organization and ministries of the church.

Part 2 provides an answer to these problems by proposing a twofold hermeneutic for church ministry. First, I will advocate some general principles for interpreting the Bible that affect the church. Second, I will discuss some special hermeneutics for conducting the church's ministry.

As we seek to establish a hermeneutic for the church and its ministries, we will look for principles that are normative. However, an explanation is necessary concerning what I mean by the term *normative,* for I will use it frequently in the following chapters. I am referring to what the Bible teaches about the church that applies to all people, everywhere, and at all times. In other words, these practices and principles are just as binding on the church today as they were thousands of years ago.

Section One

General Hermeneutics for Interpreting the Bible

In chapter 2 of part 1, we examined several general hermeneutical principles for interpreting the Bible. In chapters 3 and 4, I will develop two more fundamental guidelines. They not only are important for interpreting the Bible as a whole but also are vital for understanding and applying the passages that deal specifically with how churches conduct their ministries.

Chapter 3 discusses the concept of authorial intent. I will argue that the Bible means what its writers intended it to mean. This truth is especially critical for understanding both the book of Acts and the letters of Paul, both of which address church ministry. Chapter 4 explores biblical genre and how the literary content of Acts (which is historical narrative) affects our understanding of the ministry of the early church.

3

The Concept of Authorial Intent

What does a particular passage of Scripture mean? This can be determined by discovering what the human author of the passage wanted to say. This statement recognizes that the Holy Spirit worked ✓ through people to record God's message for humankind. The emphasis of this principle is on how God directed and controlled the human authors to communicate His inspired, inerrant Word.

To grasp the concept of authorial intent, we must first lay some groundwork. This involves probing two areas. One is to examine briefly the divine and human authorship (or dual authorship) of the Bible. The second area is to focus specifically on the human authorship in order to explore further the important concept of authorial intent.

The Dual Authorship of Scripture

Dual authorship is the view that the Bible is the product of both divine and human involvement. We begin this section with divine authorship, then move to human authorship, and finish by discussing the importance of a proper balance of the two emphases.

Divine Authorship

The Holy Spirit is the divine author of Scripture. This means that He superintended the human authors so that, using their own individual personalities, thought processes, and vocabularies, they

39

composed and recorded without error the exact words that God wanted written. Thus, the original copies of Scripture are inspired (or originating from God) and inerrant (or without error).

The primary assertion here is that God the Holy Spirit is the author of Scripture. The Godhead consists of the Father, the Son, and the Holy Spirit (Matt. 28:19). While all three persons were involved in the lives of the human authors (2 Tim. 3:16), the Spirit played a unique role in the inspiration process (2 Peter 1:21). Though He used the thoughts, vocabularies, and experiences of the human authors to produce His infallible Word, the message remains distinctly His. This is clearly taught in the following two passages.

Second Timothy 3:16

In this verse Paul wrote, "All Scripture is God-breathed and is useful for teaching, rebuking, correcting and training in righteousness, so that the man of God may be thoroughly equipped for every good work." The apostle said that God was actively involved in the revelation of His truth to the apostles and prophets who wrote it down. Though human authors actually penned the texts, God took the initiative. He thus remains the Author of the Bible, which is why it is completely authoritative and reliable.

Second Peter 1:21

How God used people to produce the Bible remains a mystery. However, we learn from this passage that no prophecy ever "had its origin in the will of man, but men spoke from God as they were carried along by the Holy Spirit." In other words, the human authors were more than just recorders of what God wanted said. The Spirit spoke through them and gave them the thoughts they uttered. Thus, God alone ultimately is responsible for what is written in Scripture.

Often commentators will illustrate this process by using a sailing metaphor. The vessel represents the biblical writers and the wind symbolizes the inspiration process. Just as a strong wind blows the sailing vessel through the water, so the Spirit moved or carried along the human writers so that they captured the divine message.

Inspiration
The fact: 2 Timothy 3:16
The process: 2 Peter 1:21

Human Authorship

Human authorship of Scripture means that God used people to put His thoughts into writing. Though the Holy Spirit is the sovereign agent in producing God's Word, the Lord in His infinite wisdom chose to work through specific individuals (such as Moses, David, and Paul) to record His message to humankind. This means that God used the thinking, talents, styles, life circumstances, and contemporary literary forms of the human authors. Rather than override these factors, He used them to communicate His timeless message.

By choosing to work through human authors, God accommodated the communication of His Word to meet the needs of people. This does not mean that God compromised on the truth in any way. Rather, He ensured that individuals from all walks of life would be able to understand and apply His inspired message.

Who Wrote the Bible?
God: the Holy Spirit
People: the human authors

Balancing the Divine and Human Authorship of Scripture

History has demonstrated the importance of keeping the divine and human authorship of Scripture in balance. In some cases, people have emphasized the divine side over the human. They have ignored such things as the human author's personal history, language, and style of writing, all of which are vital to consider when doing good exegesis.

Those who fail to take into consideration the human

authorship of Scripture spout warped interpretations that miss the true meaning of the text. This, in turn, leads to an unsound application. For example, consider the devotional approach to Bible study in which the reader randomly flips through Scripture and settles on a particular passage with no regard to its immediate or remote context. While it's possible that people can benefit at times from such an approach, they are more inclined to rip a verse out of context and foist on it a meaning never intended by God.

In other cases, people have overemphasized the human authorship of Scripture and failed to recognize that the Bible is God's inspired and authoritative Word to His people. It's assumed that Scripture is just another piece of ancient literature that reflects an outdated and flawed view of life. Supposedly the Bible is a book filled with opinions, not divine truth. Allegedly it's woefully lacking in theological content and (contrary to 2 Timothy 3:16) not particularly useful for teaching, rebuking, correcting, and training in righteousness (at least not any more than other ancient or modern writings). The postmodernist would assert, "It's great that the Bible works for you, but don't force it on me!"

Christians should reject such a low view of Scripture. The Bible says, "The word of God is living and active. Sharper than any double-edged sword, it penetrates even to dividing soul and spirit, joints and marrow; it judges the thoughts and attitudes of the heart" (Heb. 4:12).

Maintaining a Balance

Divine Authorship   Human Authorship

Authorial Intent

I have stressed that God the Holy Spirit worked through various people to write the Bible. I also have underscored the importance of maintaining a balance between the divine and human authorship of Scripture. I now want to pursue further the concept of authorial intent.[1] In this section I will present the concept, illustrate it, stress its importance, look at possible exceptions, and see how authorial intent applies to the genre of Scripture.

The Concept

Authorial intent concerns itself with discovering the meaning of Scripture. Conservative scholars maintain that the divine message in the Bible is the same as the one communicated by the human authors. In other words, there is no difference between what the human author said and what God said. The implication, of course, is that we must discover what a writer such as Moses, David, or Paul communicated in order to understand the message that God wanted to convey.

Some Illustrations

Turning a good novel into a movie is one illustration of authorial intent. Imagine reading a classic by either Charles Dickens or Mark Twain, or a modern work by either Tom Clancy or John Grisham. When these types of novels are made into films, people who have read the book will be inclined to see the movie version of it. But they're often disappointed because the screen writers have changed much of the original story so that it differs radically from what the author had penned. Of course, this is one reason why authors hesitate to turn their novels into movies. Their main intent in producing their work is lost in the shuffle of making it into a film.

Rex Koivisto provides another illustration of authorial intent. He recalls the popular song entitled "Puff the Magic Dragon," which was written by the folk musical group Peter, Paul, and Mary. It's a tune about the imaginary world of a little boy who is growing into adulthood. However, many who heard that song in the 1960s believed that the magic dragon was marijuana that the user "puffed" on. They were convinced that the song writer's intent was to communicate a message about drugs. Koivisto then relates the following story:

> Peter, Paul, and Mary had a thirty-year reunion tour, which was videotaped and later televised. Late in the program, Peter Yarrow was about to lead the audience in singing "Puff," which had since its debut become a popular American folk song. But he prefaced his remarks with an illuminating comment, to this effect: "Many people thought that this song was about drugs. But it never was. It was a simple song about a boy and his dragon, and the sorrows of leaving boyhood. I know. I'm Puff's daddy."[2]

The Importance

Discovering an author's intended meaning is important for at least three reasons. First, it's critical to good exegesis. Second, it prevents certain common errors of interpretation (such as eisegesis, allegorization, and blunders associated with devotional reading). Third, it provides a more objective means for interpreting the Bible and validating one's explanation of the text. Let's take a few moments to explore these three items in further detail.

Good Exegesis

The concept of authorial intent is important to good exegesis. This may be defined as "bringing out of the text the meaning the writers intended to convey and which their readers were expected to gather from it."[3] We can't discover what the text means unless we know what the authors meant by what they wrote. Thus, exegesis is based on authorial intent.

For example, pastors who want to know what the church can and can't do should seek to determine what Luke (who wrote Acts) and Paul (who wrote many letters) wanted to communicate in their writings. This can only be done by exegeting their works. The process involves carefully observing the grammar of the text, the author's use of words, the sequential development of the text, the history and culture behind a given passage, the literary backdrop, and so on.

For instance, let's consider an historical narrative from Acts. Exegeting this would involve studying the events that Luke, the human author, selected to communicate to his intended message. This calls for a knowledge of narrative literature. The idea is that Luke, under the sovereign control of the Holy Spirit, selected only the material that best advanced the argument of his book. Good exegesis takes this important matter into account as it seeks to discover the meaning of the passage.

Errors of Interpretation

The concept of authorial intent will help the interpreter to avoid certain common hermeneutical mistakes. The first one is eisegesis. People who argue that "You can make the Bible mean whatever you want it to mean" are referring to the practice of eisegesis. This is reading into the text ideas that are foreign to it.

A second common error is allegorization. This involves searching "for a deeper meaning in the literal statements of a text that is not readily apparent in the text itself."[4] Supposedly God has placed some higher spiritual meaning in the passage, and it's up to the reader to discover it. This implies that the literal meaning of the text is not its true meaning. Of course, this is a completely subjective way of interpreting Scripture. "The method often indicates more of the thought patterns of the interpreter than that of the original author."[5] If this approach is adopted, there's no way of validating the legitimacy of one's interpretation.

A third common interpretive error occurs when one reads the text "devotionally." What pastor doesn't encourage God's people to read the Bible for themselves? Sadly, they often force alien ideas onto a passage of Scripture. As they "devotionally" read the Bible, they resort either to allegorization or eisegesis. For instance, many read the text to discover "what it means to me" or "what I can get out of it," rather than to learn the true message being communicated by the passage. While this approach may seem harmless, it runs roughshod over the true meaning of the text. The devotional reader goes away feeling warmed but not filled, moved but not changed.

Doing Church Subjectivity

These problems (as well as others) demonstrate the dangers of a subjective approach to interpreting Scripture and the need for some guidelines or controls in determining the true meaning of the text. Otherwise Bible students will make a passage mean whatever they want (see the caution against this in 2 Peter 1:20).

Authorial intent gives interpreters objective guidelines to follow, which ensures that their interpretation is valid. The goal is to determine precisely what the human writers meant when they penned a certain portion of Scripture under the guidance of the Holy Spirit. In this approach there is no subjectivity, for the Bible is allowed to speak for itself.

Any Exceptions?

The concept of authorial intent affects how we determine the true meaning of a biblical passage. The Holy Spirit's intent is found in the writer's intent.

A Question

This point, however, raises an important question, if not an objection. Could God intend a deeper meaning in Scripture than the author's intended meaning? Stated another way, could the Bible have a second, fuller meaning that goes beyond the author's original meaning?[6]

An Answer

The answer is *yes*. Though not the norm, it seems to be the case in some limited situations. For instance, sometimes a New Testament writer's use and interpretation of an Old Testament passage might indicate that "God may intend more than was clearly intended by the human authors."[7] Another example would be prophetic literature. For instance, did Isaiah fully understand all that he was prophesying about the Messiah in Isaiah 7:14 and 9:6? It's impossible to know for sure. But there's a good likelihood he didn't comprehend all that God intended or was unaware of what we know from what is revealed in the New Testament (see 1 Peter 1:10–12). We could ask the same question of Daniel and his writings (for example, Daniel 9) and John and his writings in Revelation.

Let's give some further consideration to 1 Peter 1:10–12. Some have argued that God intended a fuller meaning than the one perceived by the Old Testament prophets regarding their prophecies of the sufferings and glory of Christ. In contrast, Peter indicated that they did have some awareness and understanding of the Messiah's afflictions and exaltation. What they didn't know was when and under what circumstances Jesus' suffering would occur.

There is a great deal of subjectivity in trying to discover a deeper meaning in the text. Who decides when there is a fuller meaning, and how is that determined? In light of this uncertainty, it is best to say that "each text of Scripture has a single meaning, though some may have related implications or . . . 'submeanings.'"[8]

A Conclusion

In some limited situations, God may have intended a fuller sense than that understood by the human author. However, we should view this as the exception rather than the rule.

The Application to Genre

Toward the end of chapter 4, I will discuss and emphasize how important the concept of authorial intent is to understanding and interpreting the historical narrative literature in Acts. Here I want to stress that we should seek the author's intent in all the genres of the Bible.

Questions for Reflection and Discussion
1. Why is it important to recognize that God wrote the Bible? How were people involved in this process?
2. Do you know of a Bible teacher or pastor who has been guilty of any of the common interpretive errors mentioned in this chapter? If so, which errors? What were the circumstances, and what were the results?
3. How does the concept of authorial intent prevent a more subjective approach of interpreting the Bible from happening?

4. Do you believe that sometimes God intends for Scripture to have a deeper sense than the human author may have intended or understood? If so, under what circumstances? How common is this? Do you usually look for a deeper meaning whenever you study the Bible?
5. How does the task of determining the authorial intent of a passage affect one's understanding of the various genres of Scripture?

Endnotes

1. The concept of authorial intent is somewhat ambiguous. However, I've chosen to use this label because people are more familiar with it than other (possibly better) tags such as *assertion* or *affirmation*. For more information on this matter, you may want to read Millard Erickson's book entitled *Evangelical Interpretation* (Grand Rapids: Baker, 1993), 31.
2. Rex A. Koivisto, *One Lord, One Faith* (Wheaton: Victor, 1993), 160.
3. F. F. Bruce, "Interpretation of the Bible," in *Evangelical Dictionary of Theology,* ed. Walter A. Elwell (Grand Rapids: Baker, 1984), 565.
4. S. E. McCleeland, "Allegory," in *Evangelical Dictionary of Theology,* ed. Walter A. Elwell (Grand Rapids: Baker, 1984), 33.
5. Ibid.
6. In scholarly circles this concept of a fuller meaning of Scripture is known as *sensus plenior,* which means "fuller sense." "The idea is that some scriptural passages may have a 'fuller sense' than intended or understood by the human author, a sense that was, however, intended by God" (Roy B. Zuck, *Basic Bible Interpretation: A Practical Guide to Discovering Biblical Truth* [Wheaton: Victor, 1991], 273).
7. Ibid., 274. See also Gordon D. Fee, *Gospel and Spirit* (Peabody, Mass.: Hendrickson, 1991), 19.
8. Zuck, *Basic Bible Interpretation,* 274–75. The writer goes on to quote the *Chicago Statement on Biblical Hermeneutics:* "We affirm that the meaning expressed in each biblical text is single, definite, and fixed....What a passage means is fixed by the author and is not subect to change by readers. This does not imply that further revelation on the subject cannot help one come to a fuller understanding, but simply that the meaning given in a text is not changed because additional truth is revealed subsequently."

4

The Importance of the Bible's Genres

The Bible is made up of numerous genres. Recognizing these literary forms affects the way one interprets a passage. In this chapter we'll first look at the overall concept of biblical genres. Then, we'll focus on the narrative genre of Acts and see how it affects our understanding of the way in which the early church conducted its ministries.

The Genres of the Bible

The following section will present a definition of *genre*, provide some examples of genres, and discuss why knowing the Bible's genres is important to its accurate interpretation.

Definition

Genre is a French word that means a literary kind or type. As you read through Scripture, you'll discover that certain books of the Bible display common characteristics that are recognizable and distinguish them from others. These common characteristics make up a distinct literary type or genre.

Examples

What are some of the different kinds of genre (or literary types) you'll find throughout the Bible? In *Basic Bible Interpretation,* Zuck presents seven broad genres found throughout the Old and New Testaments.

One example is the legal genre, and it's found in the books of the Pentateuch. Another example is the narrative genre, and it's found in the Pentateuch as well as 1 and 2 Samuel, 1 and 2 Chronicles, Ruth, and Jonah. A third example is poetry, and it's found in Job, Psalms, Proverbs, Ecclesiastes, and Song of Songs. A fourth example is the wisdom genre, and it's found in Job, Proverbs, and Ecclesiastes. A fifth example is the gospel genre, and it's found in the four Gospels. (I'll also refer to this as historical narrative literature.) A sixth example is logical discourse, and it's found in the New Testament epistles. Last is the prophetic genre, and it's found in the major and minor prophets of the Old Testament and the book of Revelation in the New Testament.[1]

Some Genres of Scripture
1. Legal genre: the books of the Pentateuch
2. Narrative genre: Pentateuch, 1 and 2 Samuel, 1 and 2 Chronicles, Ruth, Jonah
3. Poetic genre: Job, Psalms, Proverbs, Ecclesiastes, Song of Songs
4. Wisdom genre: Job, Proverbs, and Ecclesiastes
5. Gospel (or historical narrative) genre: the four Gospels
6. Logical discourse genre: the epistles of the New Testament
7. Prophetic genre: portions of the major and minor prophets, and the book of Revelation

You'll note that many books of Scripture contain more than one type of genre. For example, the Pentateuch consists of both legal and narrative literature. Job consists of both poetry and wisdom literature. Others have written on biblical genres and classified them differently. A classic text is Leland Ryken's *The Literature of the Bible.*[2]

Importance

Why are we emphasizing biblical genres? The answer is that they affect how we interpret the whole Bible and its various parts, and how we apply Scripture to the ministries of the church.

The Whole Bible

An understanding of the whole Bible's genre is important to interpreting and applying it properly. The tendency is to interpret the Bible as if it was all one type of literature. For example, many read Scripture literally, which is good in most situations. However, the Holy Spirit didn't intend us to take certain parts of the Bible literally. For example, consider the use of figurative language. The psalmist said, "For the Lord God is a sun and shield" (Ps. 84:11). Isaiah wrote, "But the wicked are like the tossing sea" (Isa. 57:20). These authors used figurative language to convey information in a picturesque and memorable way. They didn't intend their words to be taken in a crassly literal fashion.

Jesus also used figurative language. For instance, He announced in John 10:7: "I am the gate." He didn't mean that He was a movable barrier that swings open and shut, but rather the way of salvation (see v. 9). Previously Christ used a shepherding analogy to talk about His relationship with His followers (vv. 1–5). John (the writer of the fourth gospel) noted that "Jesus used this figure of speech, but they did not understand what he was telling them" (v. 6). In order to grasp what Jesus was saying, we must first recognize His use of figurative language. We then seek to discern the literal meaning behind the analogy.

Those who wish to interpret Scripture accurately must take into account the various genres of the Bible. Different literary types call for different hermeneutical approaches to interpret those forms. To be careful and accurate interpreters of God's Word, we must handle differently such genres as poetry, parables, allegories, genealogies, epistles, and narratives.

Once the interpreter knows the author's genre, an understanding of that literary type will signal how he has arranged the text and what one should notice. For example, when you read the book of Psalms, it's important to know that it is filled with poetry. The interpretation of many passages will hinge on recognizing figures of speech, different types of parallelism, and the classification of the psalm. With respect to the last item, one should ask whether it's a psalm of lament, declarative praise, descriptive praise, and so on. When you know the proper category to which the psalm belongs, this will help you figure out the structure of the passage and how the author used this arrangement of his material to communicate his message.

The New Testament

An understanding of the genre of the New Testament is important to interpreting and applying it properly. The New Testament, like the Old, consists of different genres. For instance, here are four broad literary types: Gospels, Acts, Letters, and Apocalypse.[3] These, in turn, consist of specific, diverse genres such as parables, genealogies, narratives, speeches, wisdom statements, and so on.

Most of the passages that address the church and how it functions are found in the New Testament. Thus, we'll focus specifically on how to interpret the New Testament in general and its genres in particular.

Four Broad Genres of the New Testament
1. Gospels
2. Acts
3. Letters
4. Apocalypse

The Ministries of the Church

An understanding of the epistolary and narrative genres of the New Testament is important in interpreting and applying the passages that relate specifically to the church and how it conducts its ministries. These two broad genres of the New Testament address most of the passages that affect how the church does its work. Epistolary literature consists of two groups. The first is the Pauline epistles. They include Paul's pastoral letters (1 and 2 Timothy and Titus), prison letters (Philippians, Philemon, Colossians, and Ephesians), and other letters (1 and 2 Thessalonians, 1 and 2 Corinthians, Galatians, and Romans). The second group is the general epistles. They consist of the following letters: James; Peter; Hebrews; Jude; and 1, 2, and 3 John.

The pastor needs to know the epistles and their historical context well in order to develop a sound ecclesiology. We find much pastoral theology that applies to the church in the epistles, especially Paul's pastoral letters (1 and 2 Timothy and Titus). They are indispensable to any clergyman who wants to know what God says about the church and its ministry.

The other broad New Testament genre we want to consider is historical narrative, especially the kind found in Acts. There are two reasons why it's important to know this literary type. First, it provides the historical, social, and cultural setting for many of the epistles in general and the early church in particular. We must know these settings in order to understand the epistles and apply them properly. Second, to correctly understand the theology of Acts, we must know how to interpret historical narrative. (This is one of the most difficult aspects of hermeneutics, and we'll discuss it in the next section.) If we misinterpret and misapply the material in Acts, it can adversely affect the way we conduct the ministry of the church.

Historical narratives and epistles are diverse in several ways. For one thing, they teach truth differently. Historical narratives generally convey truth by recounting key events. An author such as Luke carefully researched, selected, and arranged the various episodes that best supported the argument and intent of his book (see Luke 1:1–4; Acts 1:1–2). In contrast, the epistles generally convey truth through carefully reasoned propositions and imperatives.

More work has been done in the epistles than in historical narrative. For instance, seminary students from as late as the 1970s focused more on the epistles than on narrative literature. Perhaps this reflects the focus of the scholarly evangelical world.[4] A quick review of most seminary curricula indicates that some change has taken place. However, the emphasis is still on the epistles such as Romans, Corinthians, and so on. In pastoral theology, the emphasis is on 1 and 2 Timothy and Titus. This is due partly to the difficulty of interpreting narrative literature. Whereas the epistles are fairly straightforward in their structure, narrative material can be digressive.

The emphasis on the epistles is also problematic, for the postmodern generation responds best to preaching from the narrative portions of the New Testament. This could mean an eventual shift away from the epistles in favor of the Gospels and Acts. If this happens, it could prove as troublesome as the current trend in preaching. In either case, we need to work hard at developing hermeneutical principles for interpreting the narrative literature of the New Testament. The following section will provide five general principles, or guidelines, to accomplish this.

The Genre of Acts

I have stressed the importance of genre in general to interpret the Bible and its various parts. Now I will narrow my focus in the rest of this chapter to historical narrative, especially that of Acts. The reason is that most churches and denominations refer to this book of Scripture to support their differing ecclesiastical positions. In this regard, we need to ask and answer two key questions:

1. How do we interpret historical narrative?
2. In light of that, what applies to all churches everywhere and at all times?

I noted in chapter 2 that Gordon Fee is one of the few scholars who has addressed this area and provided some principles, or guidelines, for interpreting historical narrative and determining what is and isn't normative. In *Gospel and Spirit* and *How to Read the Bible for All It's Worth* he has influenced my thinking, and I have borrowed heavily from his teaching.[5]

The following are five critical hermeneutical principles that apply the concept of authorial intent. Knowing these will help us to interpret the historical narrative genre of Acts. This, in turn, will enable us to discover what is normative for churches today. The material that follows will also serve as the hermeneutical foundation for the final section of this chapter, which discusses the special hermeneutics of conducting the ministry of the church.

Principle #1

The author's primary intent for writing the narrative is key to interpreting his account. In other words, to properly understand and apply a passage from a book such as Acts, we must first discover the author's primary intent for writing the narrative. Knowing this will help us to understand the theology of the book and see how it affects all the material that Luke has included.

According to Acts 1:8, Luke's primary intent was to show how God used the Holy Spirit to empower His people—the church—as witnesses. They were commanded to spread the gospel from what was primarily a Jewish audience in Jerusalem to all people everywhere. Knowing this will help explain the narrative of Acts.

Principle #2

Each section of the narrative fits into and contributes to the author's primary intent. Acts consists of various sections. Our job is to determine how each section fits the overall intent of the author. We should ask, "Why did he include the material in this section of the book, and how does it contribute to and advance the overall intent?"

We have noted that Acts has a primary purpose. Likewise, each section of the book has a main intent, and this harmonizes with the overall thrust of Acts. By taking the time to understand the aim of individual sections and see how it relates to the main intent of the book, we will have a clearer understanding of the theology and emphases of Acts. For instance, the author's intent for 1:12–26 is to show the need for Spirit-empowered witnesses. In verse 8, Jesus said that the disciples would be His witnesses, including the apostles. Because of the demise of Judas, they were one short of twelve. So the disciples responded by choosing a Spirit-empowered replacement named Matthias.

Principle #3

Some narrative material is incidental and thus not as important to the book's primary intent as other material. This incidental material is found in the book as a whole and in each section in particular. The author uses this material for descriptive and sequential purposes. Though we need this information to fill in the details, it's not as crucial as other data in the book.

It would be incorrect to conclude that incidental material is less inspired than primary material. All Scripture is divinely inspired (2 Tim. 3:16). That having been said, some material is more crucial to the argument of a book than other pieces of information. The latter, while of secondary importance to the writer's primary intent, is nevertheless vital to the flow of the narrative.

The same thing could be said of the teaching value of incidental information in Acts. Primary doctrines of the faith should not be built on brief or vaguely worded comments appearing in the narrative. To overemphasize these passages would be to misunderstand the intent of Luke and distort the argument of his book.

For example, Acts 1:12–26 relates how the early church chose Matthias to replace Judas. Verse 26 specifically says that the group cast lots to make the decision. While this information is needed to understand the narrative, it is not a primary verse in the passage. Other verses are more crucial in helping us understand the message that Luke wanted to convey, namely, that Jesus' followers obeyed Him and chose a Spirit-empowered witness to replace Judas.

Principle #4

The narrative's primary material may contain normative principles for the church. We look to a book's main information to discover the author's primary intent. It's from this material that we look for normative teaching or principles that can be applied to the church today. Thus, not all the information contained in Acts is precedent setting and normative.[6] We should ask, "Was it Luke's intent by including this material to establish a precedent? Did he incorporate this information because he wanted others to

observe and implement it in their ministries?" Our job as interpreters is to make this determination by using the evidence present
in the biblical text.

For example, I don't see a timeless, normative principle in the
case of Matthias. Perhaps one might argue that the information
underscores the need for churches today to have leaders who are
Holy Spirit empowered witnesses for Christ. However, I think that
Luke would be surprised if we made that application. My view is
that the situation in Acts 1 isn't comparable to today. Luke was
dealing with the need to establish an apostolic witness for a ministry being shouldered by the Twelve (see v. 25).

Principle #5

*The narrative's incidental material doesn't include normative
principles for the church.* Unless the text indicates otherwise, the
divine and human authors didn't record incidental material for
normative purposes. In light of this, we'd be mistaken to make
secondary information normative for the church.

This incidental material, however, may add support to or illustrate a primary, normative teaching that's found in another part of
Scripture either in the same book or another book.[7] For example,
consider how Jesus' followers chose Matthias by casting of lots
(Acts 1:26). *What* they did was more important than *how* they did
it. Thus it would be mistaken to assert that the practice of casting
lots is binding on the church today. Luke wanted us to know that
the early church obeyed Scripture by continuing the apostolic witness originally established by Jesus (vv. 20, 25).[8]

Let's consider the church meeting that is mentioned in Acts
20:7. Paul, his associates, and some believers in Troas came together on the first day of the week to break bread. Most likely, this
is an example of how the early church exercised its freedom to
meet whenever it was convenient, as taught in Romans 14:5–8. In
this situation, the believers chose to meet on the first day of the
week. Of course, they could have also met on some other day of
the week. (I'll pursue this discussion further in the next section
of the book.)

Five Principles for Interpreting and Applying Biblical Narrative
1. The author's primary intent for writing the narrative is key to interpreting the account.
2. Each section of the narrative in some way fits into and contributes to the author's primary intent.
3. Some narrative material is incidental and thus not as important to the book's primary intent.
4. The narrative's primary material may contain normative principles for the church.
5. The narrative's incidental material doesn't include normative principles for churches today.

Questions for Reflection and Discussion

1. Have you received any training in the various genres of the Bible? If not, why not? If you have, what kind of training was it?
2. What has this chapter taught you about the genre of the Bible as a whole? What has it taught you about the genre of the New Testament? About the genre of Acts?
3. Do the five principles for interpreting historical narrative make sense? Explain. Do you believe that they will help you in interpreting Acts? Explain. Will you use them? Explain.
4. How will the five principles help you to understand what churches can and can't do? Can you think of any ecclesiastical practices that these principles might indicate aren't normative for churches today?

Endnotes

1. Roy B. Zuck, *Basic Bible Interpretation: A Practical Guide to Discovering Biblical Truth* (Wheaton: Victor, 1991), 126–35.
2. Leland Ryken, *The Literature of the Bible* (Grand Rapids: Zondervan, 1974).
3. Walter L. Liefeld, *Interpreting the Book of Acts* (Grand Rapids: Baker, 1995), 9.
4. Much to its credit, the pastoral ministries department at Dallas Theological Seminary, where I received my training, realized that its

students must preach from the narrative portions of the Old Testament and New Testament. So it began to probe narrative literature in the 1970s.

5. Gordon D. Fee, *Gospel and Spirit: Issues in New Testament Hermeneutics* (Peabody, Mass.: Hendrickson, 1991); and Gordon D. Fee and Douglas Stuart, *How to Read the Bible for All It's Worth* (Grand Rapids: Zondervan, 1981).

6. Others agree. See Jack Kuhatschek, *Applying the Bible* (Grand Rapids: Zondervan, 1990), 68–69; and Fee and Stuart, *How to Read the Bible for All It's Worth,* 68.

7. See Kuhatschek, *Applying the Bible,* 120.

8. It is not clear from the context that this was a meeting of the church (cf. my comments on p. 72). However, for the sake of the argument, I will assume that it was.

Section Two

Special Hermeneutics for Church Ministry

In chapters 3 and 4 of part 2, we covered two general hermeneutical principles that are vital to interpreting the Bible as a whole and especially passages that address the ministries of the church. In chapters 5 through 8, we will discuss some special, or particular, hermeneutical principles that serve as guidelines for conducting the ministries of the church.

The format of each chapter is essentially the same. A chapter will begin by posing a particular hermeneutical issue in the form of a question. The rest of the chapter then will answer that question and conclude with a normative principle for the church.

5

The Negative Versus
the Positive Hermeneutic

In this chapter, we pose the question: "What's the role of the New Testament in determining ministry practices?" Specifically, must we find our church practices in the New Testament? There are two answers to these questions. One is the negative hermeneutic and the other is the positive hermeneutic. This chapter will present both and determine which is correct, thereby providing a normative principle to be used by churches today.

The Negative Hermeneutic

The negative hermeneutic presents one answer to the question, "Must we find our church practices in the New Testament?"[1] I will first articulate this position, then present the arguments for it, and finally evaluate it.

The Position

The negative hermeneutic argues that if a practice isn't found in the Bible, then we can't do it. The following motto states this position well: "Where the Bible speaks, we speak; and where the Bible is silent, we're silent." The issue is one of presence or absence. According to figure 1, if you can find such and such in the Bible, it's permissible. However, if the practice isn't mentioned somewhere in Scripture, it's forbidden.

Presence: You can find _____ in the Bible; thus, you can do it.

Absence: You can't find _____ in the Bible; thus, you can't do it.

Figure 1

The Support

The support for the negative hermeneutic is based on what is and what isn't considered scriptural. (Only that which is found in God's Word is considered biblical.) Proponents of this view ✓believe that the Bible provides a complete picture of how the early church organized itself and conducted its ministries. This is described in various apostolic commands and practices. Therefore, God's Word reveals all that we need to know about the church, its organization, and its ministries. Thus, what we do in our churches must be based on that information, especially if our ministries are to be biblical. If a church practice is biblical, one should be able to find support for it in Scripture. Conversely, if a church practice can't be found in God's Word, it's unbiblical and must be discontinued.

Some Examples

The following church practices are a sampling of what are considered unbiblical activities because one supposedly can't find them in Scripture. I'm not aware of any particular church that negates all of these practices. They provide a cumulative representation of the beliefs and viewpoints of several different churches.

One tabooed practice is instrumental music. Since the New Testament is silent about the use of musical instruments in the early church, we supposedly can't use them in worship today. This includes not only drums and guitars but also pianos and organs.

A second forbidden practice is church membership. Allegedly no evidence exists in the New Testament for the standard modern routine of requiring people to join a congregation. Consequently, joining a local church, keeping a membership roll, and asking people to meet certain conditions for membership are unbiblical and antithetical to what is taught in Scripture.

A third banned practice is congregational voting. Since voting on church matters can't be found in the Bible, it's reputedly unscriptural to follow this practice. (Those who permit congregational voting argue that it's their right and privilege to do so as believer priests; see 1 Peter 2:5, 9).

A fourth tabooed practice is allowing one pastor to lead the church. It's argued that a form of church government with only one elder, or pastor, is not found anywhere in the New Testament. Supposedly the leadership of the early church involved a plurality of elders.

A fifth forbidden practice is membership in a denomination. Not only is the New Testament allegedly silent on denominations, but also the congregations in the first century A.D. were autonomous. (Detractors would argue that these churches weren't autonomous, based on such passages as Acts 15:23–29 and 16:4–5.)

A sixth banned practice is drama. The standard argument is that because acting isn't in the Bible, it can't be done in church. After all, the Greeks used drama, and the church must have known about it. Yet they refused to permit it in their congregations. Likewise, so should churches today.

> **Some So-Called Unbiblical Church Practices**
> 1. Instrumental music
> 2. Church membership
> 3. Congregational voting
> 4. One-man pastorate
> 5. Denominations
> 6. Drama

An Evaluation

We've just considered the argument for the negative hermeneutic and looked at some examples of church practices that reputedly are unbiblical. It's now time to evaluate this method of interpretation. Though it might initially seem to make sense, it won't stand up under scrutiny. The negative hermeneutic is inaccurate for at least four reasons.

The Negative Hermeneutic Is Based on a Non Sequitur *Argument*[2]

Simply because a practice isn't found in the Bible doesn't mean that we either should or should not do it, or even prohibit its practice in churches today. For example, a city's legal codes say nothing about whether it's permissible for me to cook hot dogs on the grill in my backyard. They simply don't address the issue. But according to the logic of the negative hermeneutic, I can't cook hot dogs in my backyard. After all, it's not mentioned in the city legal codes. Therefore the practice must be wrong, and I shouldn't do it.

Just because a certain practice isn't mentioned anywhere in the Bible (this is called an argument from silence) doesn't mean that the church can't do it. Absence of proof isn't proof of absence. Common sense tells us that some of the things the early church practiced weren't mentioned previously in Scripture. (At that time believers principally used the Old Testament.) For example, some New Testament believers met for corporate worship "on the first day of every week" (1 Cor. 16:2). Yet this practice would have been different from what God's people did in Old Testament times. (They would have gathered on the Sabbath.) If we followed the logic of the negative hermeneutic, churches today would possibly have to abandon the practice of corporately worshiping on Sunday!

Let's consider the objection to using instrumental music in worship. The argument is that because it's nowhere mentioned in the Bible, it shouldn't be done. Koivisto counters with the following remark: "All it would prove is that they *did* not use them, not that they *should* not have used them. If they did not use them, there may have been any number of reasons for such: lack of availability, lack of time for musical creativity due to persecution, or lack of permanent meeting locations. We simply do not know."[3]

The Negative Hermeneutic Can't Be Practiced Consistently

No one can be consistent in his or her practice of the negative hermeneutic. Why? Because there are some things that even proponents of this view do which aren't affirmed in Scripture. Imagine someone in this group arriving at church early. He flips on a light switch and then turns on the air conditioner. Yet neither of these practices are mentioned in Scripture. Are we to conclude that using lights and air conditioners is unbiblical? Of course not!

After I graduated from college and completed a tour of duty with the Navy, I decided to teach school until I could save enough money to attend seminary. One of the other teachers went to a church that embraced the negative hermeneutic. For instance, they believed that using instruments in corporate worship was unscriptural. One day I asked whether his church used microphones or hymnals. He said that they did. It was all I could do to refrain from asking him where his church found these practices affirmed in the Bible. Though they are not mentioned in God's Word, his church still made use of these devices. Now that's being inconsistent!

My point isn't that the church should be absolutely consistent in its practices. (In fact, that would be asking the impossible.) The issue is that the negative hermeneutic can't be followed consistently. After all, we do things in church that aren't addressed in the Bible but are acceptable due to historical, cultural, and technological developments. Some examples are the use of a nursery, paved parking lots, first aid kits, computers, and so on. Consequently, those who advocate the negative hermeneutic can't practice it consistently. Instead, they're left with a pick-and-choose approach to reputedly "sanctioned" ministries of the church.

The Negative Hermeneutic Eliminates All Parachurch Ministries

The negative hermeneutic argues that parachurch organizations aren't found in the Bible and therefore are unbiblical. Parachurch groups are religious organizations that work alongside the local church to promote the cause of Christ. They may have originated with the Pietists in 1669. But a large number were established in the United States in the decades following World War II. Included in this category would be: mission organizations; Christian colleges, universities, and seminaries; ministries to children, adolescents, college students, and international students; counseling ministries; and Christian publishing enterprises (to name a few).

The negative hermeneutic would mean that all forms of parachurch ministry must be eliminated. While some advocates hold this view, the majority reject it. Thus, the majority is guilty of being inconsistent.

The Negative Hermeneutic Leads to a Judgmental Spirit

The negative hermeneutic can easily lead to a judgmental spirit. Once people appoint themselves as critics of others, it's relatively easy for them to become overly harsh and condemning of what others do. They become characterized by an anti-membership, anti-parachurch, anti-voting, and anti-clericalism mentality.

Gradually a cynical spirit will spread like gangrene throughout the church and divest it of vitality and life. The goal is to play the role of Grand Inquisitor for all churches. Perhaps James had this problem in mind when he wrote, "There is only one Lawgiver and Judge, the one who is able to save and destroy. But you—who are you to judge your neighbor?" (James 4:12).

**Some Fallacies of
the Negative Hermeneutic**
1. It's based on a *non sequitur* argument.
2. It can't be practiced consistently.
3. It eliminates parachurch ministries.
4. It easily leads to a judgmental spirit.

The Positive Hermeneutic

Considering all the problems with the negative hermeneutic, we should look to the positive hermeneutic for a biblical answer to the question, "Must we find our church practices in the New Testament?" I'll first articulate this position, then discuss the issue of what it means to be biblical, and finally relate some examples of the positive hermeneutic.

The Position

The positive hermeneutic argues that though a practice isn't found in the Bible, we are still free to perform it as long as it doesn't differ with or contradict in any way the clear teaching √ of Scripture. This qualification is imperative, for God's Word is always the final authority regarding what the church can and can't do.

The positive hermeneutic emphasizes the church's freedom to choose practices that don't contradict Scripture. Rather than argue that we can't practice what's not found in the Bible, it makes more sense to maintain that God gives us freedom to do or not do what Scripture doesn't mention. Though the Bible is silent about many contemporary church practices, this doesn't mean they are taboo. The key factor is whether a practice is banned in Scripture. Just because the text is silent on a particular issue doesn't mean it is prohibited.

The Issue

The negative hermeneutic raises the issue, What does it mean to be biblical? It argues that to be biblical something must be found in the Bible. That's true. For example, for something to be Shakespearean, it must be found in the writings of Shakespeare.

But the advocate for the negative hermeneutic says that such practices as instrumental music, church membership, and congregational voting are wrong because Scripture is silent about them. We previously noted that this way of thinking is inconsistent, for there are other contemporary practices that also aren't mentioned in the Bible (such as the use of electric lights and air conditioners). Ultimately, the issue is not whether the Bible discusses a certain activity but rather whether it contradicts the teaching of God's Word.

Yes, it's true that many contemporary church practices are not mentioned in Scripture. But that doesn't mean they're

impermissible. We believe that every word of the Bible is true
√ (Ps. 119:160). Yet not every truth in the world is recorded in
Scripture. For example, scientists have discovered that smoking
is dangerous to your health. Yet you won't find that information
in the Bible. Similarly, dentists have discovered that you get
fewer cavities if you brush your teeth regularly. Yet again you
won't find that fact in Scripture.

It stands to reason that just as not every truth in the world is
found in the Bible, so too not every permissible church practice is
mentioned in Scripture. Rather than get uptight about what truth
or practice isn't found in the Bible, we should be praising God for
√ what He has graciously revealed to us in His Word, for apart from
His truth we couldn't function.

Again, the issue is not whether a particular practice is (or
isn't) mentioned in the Bible. Rather, it's whether it contradicts
the teaching of Scripture. The challenge for us is to think biblically so that we won't be "tossed back and forth by the waves,
and blown here and there by every wind of teaching and by the
cunning and craftiness of men in their deceitful scheming" (Eph.
4:14). We should regularly ask ourselves, "Does this practice
bring glory to God?"

Some Examples

One example is the use of musical instruments in worship. The
positive hermeneutic would argue that it's permissible to do this
as long as it doesn't violate God's Word (and it doesn't). This means
it's permissible to use musical instruments that are popular in the
American churches (such as guitars and drums) as well as those
that are popular in European churches (such as pipe organs, pianos, stringed instruments, and brass instruments). A church is
even free to exercise its liberty by opting for a pipe organ over
drums and guitars. However, it would be wrong to argue that one
instrument is more biblical than the other, for that isn't true.

A similar argument could be made for congregational voting,
church membership, the leadership of a pastor, and the existence
of a denomination. We have the freedom to permit these even

though they aren't specifically mentioned in Scripture. Our focus is not on what is either present or absent from the Bible; rather, our concern is the normative teaching of God's Word on any and all matters related to the ministry of the church.

The Normative Guideline

The following is the normative principle or guideline for the church: Believers are free to follow practices that are not found in the Bible as long as they don't contradict Scripture in any way. God's Word is the final authority in these matters!

Questions for Reflection and Discussion

1. When it comes to the ministry practices of your church, have you ever embraced the negative hermeneutic? If yes, what were the short- and long-term results?
2. Can you think of any churches that hold to a negative hermeneutic? If so, how has this affected their ministry? In what ways do they tend to be inconsistent in their interpretation and application of Scripture?
3. What are some of your church's ministry practices that you can't find in the Bible? Do they differ with or contradict Scripture? Do you believe that it's okay to permit these practices? Why or why not?
4. What parachurch ministries do you know about? Should they be allowed to exist even though they aren't specifically mentioned in the Bible? Explain.
5. What does it mean when we say that a church must be biblical in its organization and practices? In what way is your church biblical in what it does?

Endnotes

1. Rex Koivisto coined the phrase *negative hermeneutic* in his book entitled *One Lord, One Faith* (Wheaton: Victor, 1993), 169.
2. A *non sequitur* argument is one in which the conclusion doesn't follow from the evidence.
3. Koivisto, *One Lord, One Faith,* 236.

6

The Descriptive Versus the Prescriptive Hermeneutic

The following is a major question facing contemporary Christians: "Are certain first-century ministry practices normative for churches today simply because they appear in the Bible?" For example, some portions of the New Testament are descriptive, and thus present or describe the ministry practices of churches in the first century. Other passages are prescriptive and, thus, enjoin certain practices. A question arises from this: "Must the church follow the descriptive as well as the prescriptive passages in its ministry?" To put it another way, "Do all biblical passages—whether descriptive or prescriptive in nature—mandate the ministries of the church?"

This chapter will address these questions. I have divided it into two parts. The first will discuss the descriptive passages and their affect on the ministries of the church. I have labeled this discussion the descriptive hermeneutic. The second part will address the prescriptive passages, namely, those that enjoin specific ministries of the church. I have labeled this discussion the prescriptive hermeneutic. I end the chapter with a normative principle, or guideline, for the church.

The Descriptive Hermeneutic
What affect do the descriptive portions of the New Testament have on the ministry practices of churches today? One answer is that these passages are normative for all churches. In other words,

they apply not only to the churches of the first century but also to all congregations at all times, in all locations, and in all situations. In this section, I will articulate this position, define descriptive passages, show the evidence in support of this view, provide some examples, and then evaluate it.

The Position

The descriptive hermeneutic maintains that all churches, everywhere, and at all times are obligated to follow not only the prescriptive passages of the New Testament but also the descriptive passages. In other words, what the church did in the first century is to be practiced by congregations today.

The Definition

Descriptive passages are portions of Scripture that describe or relate some of the ministry practices of the early church. These passages help to tell the account of the early church. They also show us how the first-century congregations functioned and how they carried out their ministries. For instance, we find descriptive material in Acts. Luke used the historical narrative genre to relate how the early church grew and developed. We can also find descriptive passages in other books of the New Testament, especially the epistles.

The various writers of Scripture provided this information for narrative purposes. Their true-to-life descriptions of events in the early church help give us a fuller understanding of what God was doing among believers. For example, Luke wrote Acts to show how God used the church as a powerful witness to spread the gospel and reach all humankind (both Jew and Gentile) for Christ. Each section of the book contributes in some way to this intent. The descriptive passages help to flesh out the document and give it substance.

The Support

Those who embrace the descriptive hermeneutic argue that the church today should observe these descriptive passages for at least three reasons. First, since they are found in Scripture, they must biblical. And since they're biblical, we are obligated to observe them in our churches. Second, the Bible is our sole guide in matters of both faith and practice. If we can trust Scripture for our doctrine (namely, what we believe), then we can also trust God's Word for our church practices. Third, the early church set a historical precedent for all the future congregations. Thus, all we need to know about church ministry is found in the Bible. Both examples as well as commands take on normative import.

Some Examples

Now that we have discussed what descriptive passages are and how they function, lets consider some examples from Scripture. I have organized these examples around what the early church did, when it met, how it met, and how it was led.

What the Early Church Did

We can gain valuable insight by considering what the early church did when it met. For example, Acts 2:42–47 says that when the followers of Christ in Jerusalem gathered together, they devoted themselves to the apostles' teaching, fellowship, breaking of bread, prayer, sharing things in common, worship, and evangelism. The prophets, teachers, and other members of the church at Syrian Antioch practiced worship and fasting (13:2). They also sent out missionaries (v. 3). The church at Corinth held unstructured meetings in which they sang hymns and exercised spiritual gifts such as speaking in tongues and prophesying (1 Cor. 14:26–32).

Many churches observed the Lord's Supper when they met. In Acts 2:42, 46, and 20:7, Luke referred to the "breaking of bread." Walter Liefeld comments, "It isn't clear whether the 'breaking of bread' is the Lord's Supper or just a fellowship meal." He concludes that "in the absence of any other references in Acts to the practice instituted by the Lord Jesus, it can be assumed to be included in the term 'breaking of bread.'"[1]

Consequently, if the "breaking of bread" mentioned in Acts

2:46 is the Lord's Supper, then the Jerusalem church observed Communion every day. Also, if the reference in 20:7 is to a church at Troas, then they observed the Lord's Supper when they met on the first day of the week. Though not explicit, the reference to the Lord's Supper in 1 Corinthians 11:20 could indicate that the church at Corinth celebrated this ordinance when they met.

At points my statements are tentative and conditional. This is because God chose not to leave us with a precise blueprint of what the early church did. This is an important fact to remember when we evaluate the descriptive hermeneutic.

Some Early-Church Practices
1. Apostles' teaching
2. Fellowship
3. Prayer
4. Sharing possessions
5. Worship
6. Evangelism
7. Singing hymns
8. Speaking in tongues
9. Prophesying
10. Fasting
11. Breaking of bread

When the Early Church Met

Some practices concern when the early church met. For example, Acts 2:46 says that the Jerusalem congregation assembled every day in the temple courts. Whether this routine continued throughout the life of the fellowship is unknown.

It's unclear whether the event that took place in Acts 20:7–12 was the meeting of a church at Troas. The term "we" in verse 7 refers to Paul and his associates. However, the mention of other believers suggests that members of the congregation were also present. If we assume that verse 7 is a descriptive reference to the church at Troas,[2] then it met on the first day of the week. (At least it did this time.) Whether this was a continual practice isn't clear from the text. It's also possible that the church at Corinth and the churches in Galatia met on the first day of the week. However, F. F. Bruce wrote concerning verse 7, "there is no explicit reference to a Christian gathering, though it may well be implied."[3]

Some use the possible church meeting at Troas to argue that not only did the congregation meet on the first day of the week but also that it met at night. Thus, the official meeting was not during the day but rather at night. Such a conclusion, however, is far from certain. There's no question that a group of believers in Troas met that particular night. But when did their meeting begin? Regrettably, the text doesn't say. All we know is that Paul "kept on talking until midnight" (v. 7) and did not stop "until daylight" (v. 11). Perhaps the meeting began during the day and lasted until early the following morning.

How the Early Church Met

Some assume that the early church gathered primarily on Sunday morning in a large group meeting (as opposed to small group meetings) for corporate worship. If this is our assumption, we're guilty of eisegesis, not exegesis, for we're reading our modern day practice back into that of the early church. Others presume that the typical early church was small. But in reality, these congregations were quite large (see 1:13–15; 2:41; 4:4; 5:14–15; 6:1; 9:31; 11:21, 24; 14:1, 21; 16:5; 17:4, 12; 18:8, 10; 19:26; 21:20).

In *One Lord, One Faith*, Rex Koivisto demonstrates from the New Testament that the early church existed and functioned at two levels.[4] One was the large city-church meeting (Acts 2:46, 5:42, and possibly 20:20). An example is the sizable Jerusalem congregation that met together in the temple courts (2:46) or Solomon's Colonnade (3:11, 5:12). When Paul wrote to various churches located at Rome, Corinth, and so on, he was directing his letters to the large city-church in these locations.

The other level was the house-church meeting that gathered

more frequently. Probably much of the ministry of the church was carried on in these smaller home gatherings. Scripture refers to them in Acts 2:46; 12:12–17; Romans 16:3–5, 14–15 ("all the saints with them"); 1 Corinthians 16:19; Colossians 4:15; and Philemon 1–2. For example, when Paul wrote to the larger "city-church," the letter was typically circulated through these smaller "house-churches" (Col. 4:16).

In light of all this Koivisto writes, "The 'local congregation' of today, when viewed in this light, is not the same as, say the 'local congregation' of Corinth. The local congregation of today is simply a larger version of a first-century house-church in a given city and likely developed as owners gave their homes to the use of the church by moving out."[5]

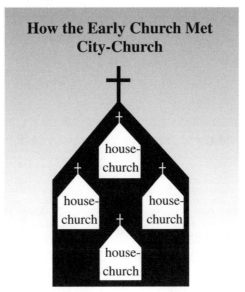

How the Early Church Was Led

It appears that many of the churches in the first century A.D. were led by a plurality of elders (in addition to the apostles). For instance, this was true of the churches in the following locations: Syrian Antioch (Acts 11:30); Derbe, Lystra, and Iconium (14:23); Ephesus (20:17); Philippi (Phil. 1:1); Pontus, Galatia, Cappadocia,

Asia, and Bithynia (1 Peter 1:1, 5:1); and those scattered among the nations (James 5:14). If elders are being talked about in 1 Thessalonians 5:12 and Hebrews 13:17, then they were leaders with authority. Since the church met at two different levels, these elders most likely led the house-churches.[6] Consequently, each city-church had a plurality of elders, but each house-church was probably led by one elder.

Acts 15 relates an incident in which the apostles and elders met in Jerusalem to consider whether it was necessary for Gentiles to observe the Mosaic law, including the rite of circumcision. Leaders from several different congregations (possibly house-churches) attended the conference. While there was a plurality of church leaders, James issued the summary directive (v. 13). Apparently he was the primary leader of the Jerusalem city-church (see 12:17; 21:18).

The Evaluation

We've stated the argument for the descriptive hermeneutic, defined descriptive passages, provided some examples, and shown the evidence in support of this view. Now let's carefully evaluate it. We'll see that there are six reasons why this interpretive approach is flawed.

Reason #1

The fact that the New Testament describes a church practice doesn't make it mandatory. For example, advocates of the descriptive hermeneutic hold some but not all descriptive church practices as mandatory. The latter include selecting leaders by lot (Acts 1), holding all things in common, selling one's possessions to help others in the church (2:44–45; 4:34–35), and baptism for the dead (1 Cor. 15:29).[7] This is inconsistent!

It is a *non sequitur* for the descriptive hermeneutic to draw universal norms from particular events. Just because an incident occurred doesn't mean that we must make it a norm for all churches everywhere. (Otherwise, why don't we try meeting in synagogues, shake out our clothes in protest, and so on, as first-century believers did? See Acts 18:1–6). We must look for the broader principles first and then illustrate and support them with the particular descriptive events, not vice versa.

The mere presence of a particular practice in the early church doesn't imply that it is a universal and timeless obligation for all churches. Advocates of the descriptive hermeneutic are guilty of making false analogies and of turning nonabsolutes into absolutes.[8]

Reason #2

Mandatory practices are prescribed in the Bible. In contrast, Scripture does not make descriptive passages into unbending commands. For example, though a number of churches had a plurality of elders, nowhere is this practice commanded! Alexander Strauch is an author who holds to the descriptive hermeneutic and the oversight of each church by a plurality of elders. However, his comments on this practice are most instructive. He writes, "There are sufficient New Testament examples and instructions to fully justify insistence on spiritual oversight by a plurality of elders; yet there is no command from the Lord, 'Thou shalt have a plurality of elders.'"[9]

Strauch gives two reasons for his statement. First, he believes that the New Testament isn't written as some law book like the Pentateuch. Second, many churches wouldn't be able to establish and maintain a plurality of elders because they don't have believers who are qualified to serve in this capacity.[10]

Incidentally, Strauch's second reason is based on a pragmatic, not a theological, consideration. Most likely, Paul's use of the words "as I directed you" in Titus 1:5 indicates that he commanded Titus to appoint elders in certain towns. They, in turn, would become the pastors of those house-churches.

Reason #3

Descriptive practices most often relate what took place in one particular church, but not necessarily in other congregations, and certainly not in all churches. For example, the church at Troas may have regularly met on the first day of the week to break bread

(Acts 20:7). Or it may be that this was an impromptu gathering to accommodate the travel plans of Paul and his associates. In either case, it's both a faulty assumption and *non sequitur* reasoning to insist that their practice represents a binding and timeless command for all churches to heed.

Reason #4

There must be evidence in these descriptive passages that the author was establishing a precedent. If there is not, then we have no business setting one. For example, was Luke's intent in Acts 20:7 to establish a normative meeting time for all churches? The answer is no. The narrative provides incidental contextual information surrounding the circumstance involving Eutychus. Luke's intent was not to establish a fixed meeting time for the church. Rather, as Acts 1:8 makes clear, the writer wanted to show how the Lord was powerfully at work in the early church to spread the gospel.

Reason #5

We must seek interpretive consistency between passages within genres (epistolary with epistolary and narrative with narrative) and between genres (epistolary with narrative and vice versa). When we compare Scripture with Scripture, we may discover that certain passages from other parts of the Bible serve to clarify an incorrect interpretation we have adopted. For example, Romans 14:5–8 teaches that believers have freedom to determine when they will gather together to worship God corporately. In light of this, it would be incorrect to conclude (as some have done) that church meeting times are being mandated in Acts 2:46 and 20:7. Rather, these congregations were simply exercising their God-given freedom to gather together for worship at a time and place most convenient for them. These two verses are illustrations of how the early church conducted ministry. In contrast, Romans 14:5–8 states a timeless principle to be observed by all believers everywhere.

Reason #6

If what is described in a narrative portion of Scripture isn't directly related to the author's intent, then it's incidental and not normative. (This is the fifth principle mentioned in chapter 4 for interpreting and applying biblical narrative material.) Unless the text indicates otherwise, the divine and human authors didn't record incidental material for normative purposes. In light of this, we'd be mistaken to make secondary information normative for the church. This incidental material, however, may add support to or illustrate a primary, normative teaching that's found in another part of Scripture either in the same book or another book.[11]

Evaluation of the Descriptive Hermeneutic

1. The fact that the New Testament describes a church practice doesn't make it mandatory.
2. Mandatory practices are prescribed or commanded in the Bible.
3. Descriptive passages relate the practices of one church but not necessarily all churches.
4. There must be evidence in a descriptive passage that the author was establishing a precedent.
5. Church practices recorded in descriptive portions may only illustrate or support principles clearly taught in other passages.
6. When what is mentioned in a descriptive portion isn't directly related to an author's intent, it's incidental rather than normative.

The Prescriptive Hermeneutic

What role do prescriptive passages serve in interpreting the Bible? Are they normative? To answer these questions, I will define the prescriptive position, discuss how to recognize prescriptive passages, identify two kinds of passages, and provide several examples for consideration.

The Definition

Prescriptive passages are divine precepts that address and dictate how churches are to conduct their ministries.[12] Whereas descriptive passages are in most cases incidental and of secondary importance,[13] prescriptive passages record directives that are of primary importance for the universal body of Christ.[14] The church is obligated to follow the prescriptive but not the descriptive passages addressing ministry.

The Recognition

What makes a passage in the Bible prescriptive? We can spot one in two ways.

Commands or Imperatives Signal Prescriptive Passages

Prescriptive passages contain commands or imperatives. The New Testament presents them in at least five different ways.

One way is the imperative mood. This is the inflectional verb form that the New Testament uses to state a command.[15] Prescriptive passages consist primarily of narrative and epistolary imperatives. Liefeld comments that there are 124 imperatives in Acts alone.[16] An example of a narrative imperative is Matthew 28:19: "Therefore go and make disciples." An example of an epistolary imperative is the command in 1 Corinthians 11:24–25 regarding the Lord's Supper: "Do this in remembrance of me."

A second way is the subjunctive mood.[17] One form of this is the hortatory subjunctive. It expresses a command in the first person that exhorts people to action.[18] An example is 2 Corinthians 7:1, where Paul exhorts the Corinthian church, "Let us purify ourselves."

A third way is the infinitive, of which several kinds exist. One is the infinitive of command, where the writer uses an infinitive in such a way that it has the force of an imperative.[19] An example is Acts 20:28, where the NIV translates the infinitive *to shepherd* as an imperative: "Be shepherds of the church of God." Another example is 1 Corinthians 5:5, where the NIV translates the infinitive *to hand over* as an imperative: "Hand this man over."

A fourth way is the participle. When a certain kind of participle[20] is used with a verb that's in the imperative mood, the former may also take the imperative mood.[21] An example is the participle *going* in Matthew 28:19, which is translated "go" in the NIV. It's used alongside the Greek verb translated "make disciples," which is in the imperative mood. A similar situation exists in Hebrew 10:25, where the NIV translates the participle *giving up* as an imperative: "Let us not give up meeting together."[22] Finally, some participles have the force of an imperative.[23] (Admittedly, this is rare.) For example, in 2 Corinthians 8:24, Paul used the participle *showing* to command the Corinthians, "Therefore show these men the proof of your love."

A fifth way is verb tense. Sometimes the future tense carries the force of an imperative.[24] For example, Paul used the future tense as an imperative in Romans 7:7, where he cited the commandment, "Do not covet."[25]

Certain Verbs Signal Prescriptive Passages

Another way we can spot a prescriptive passage is by looking for certain kinds of Greek verbs in the biblical text. The following material discusses five examples that may signal a prescriptive passage.

One example is the use of the Greek verb *dei.* The NIV translates it as "must be" in 1 Timothy 3:2: "Now the overseer must be above reproach," and "ought" in verse 15: "If I am delayed, you will know how people ought to conduct themselves in God's household."[26] A second example is the use of *paraggello,* which the NIV translates as "we command" in 2 Thessalonians 3:6: "In the name of the Lord Jesus Christ, we command you, brothers, to keep away from every brother who is idle."

A third example is the use of *boulemai,* which the NIV translates as "I want" in 1 Timothy 2:8: "I want men everywhere to lift up holy hands in prayer."[27] A fourth example is the use of *diamarturomai,* which the NIV translates as "I charge" in 1 Timothy 5:21: "I charge you in the sight of God . . . to keep these instructions." A fifth example is *diatasso,* which the NIV translates as "directed" in Titus 1:5: "and appoint elders in every town, as I directed you."

An ability to sight read the Greek New Testament would enable you to identify these and other similar verbs when they appear in the text. However, the non-Greek reader can usually spot them in a good English translation (see the following chart). Their presence in a text doesn't mean that a writer is using them prescriptively. Thus, you will need to examine carefully the passages in the context in which they appear.

Greek Verbs That May Signal Prescriptive Passages

1. *Dei:* "Now the overseer *must be* above reproach"
   (1 Tim. 3:2).
2. *Paraggello:* "In the name of the Lord Jesus Christ, we command you, brothers" (2 Thess. 3:6).
3. *Boulemai:* "I want men everywhere to lift up holy hands in prayer, without anger" (1 Tim. 2:8).
4. *Diamarturomai:* "I charge you in the sight of God" (1 Tim. 5:21).
5. *Diatasso:* "and appoint elders . . . as I directed you" (Titus 1:5).

Two Kinds of Imperatives

Though prescriptive passages take the form of imperatives, not all imperatives are normative for churches today. Consequently, I have divided the commands of Scripture into universal imperatives and local, or limited, imperatives. Let's take a look at each.

Universal Imperatives

Universal imperatives are the first type of command. They are broad and general in scope but not always absolute in their application. They are normative for all churches everywhere at all times. You can determine whether an imperative is universal by carefully examining it within the context of a passage. The following are examples of prescriptive verses that are universal imperatives:

- It's imperative that the church make disciples (Matt. 28:19–20).
- The church must meet together regularly (Heb. 10:25).
- The church must observe the ordinances of baptism and the Lord's Supper (Matt. 26:26–29; 28:19; Acts 2:38; 1 Cor. 11:23–26).
- The church must discipline its wayward members (Matt. 18:15–17; 1 Cor. 5:1–5).
- The church must teach Scripture (2 Tim. 4:2).
- The church must evangelize the lost (Matt. 28:19; Mark 16:15).
- The church must obey its leaders (Heb. 13:17).

Local or Limited Imperatives

The second type of command is local or limited imperatives. In contrast to universal imperatives, they are specific and personal. Most often you will find them in passages of Scripture where there is an abundance of individual references and instructions (for example, the personal greetings recorded in Rom. 16; and the personal requests recorded in 1 Cor. 16:5–24).[28]

These imperatives are personal in nature, for they address specific individuals living during a particular time in history. Therefore, they are prescriptive for that time and place only. For example, Paul wrote Timothy, "Do your best to come to me quickly" (2 Tim. 4:9). In verse 13 the apostle said, "When you come, bring the cloak that I left with Carpus at Troas, and my scrolls, especially the parchments." The apostle was facing the prospect of execution by the Roman government, and he wanted his beloved son in the faith to visit him as soon as he could.

Obviously we can't obey this directive, for it doesn't pertain to us. While passages such as these may give us insight into an author and his relationship with other believers, the verses are not universal imperatives that all churches and believers must heed down through the centuries.

> **Two Kinds of Imperatives**
> 1. *Universal Imperatives*: Normative for today
> 2. *Local Imperatives*: Normative only at the time they were written

Prescriptive Passages and Wisdom

Some passages aren't prescriptive in nature; nevertheless, it is wise to emulate them. For example, many city-churches in the first century A.D. had a plurality of elders. Scripture doesn't mandate that congregations have a plurality of elders. However, wisdom teaches us that such a practice might be prudent to heed (Prov. 11:14; Eccl. 4:9–10).[29]

Team ministry is another noteworthy example. Such ministers as Paul typically ministered as part of a team (Acts 11:22–30; 13:2–3, 5; 15:40; 16:1–3). However, the Bible doesn't mandate team ministry. Nevertheless, it's generally wise to minister through teams, whether the ministry is a plurality of elders in a local church or a staff of leaders in a parachurch organization (Prov. 15:22; 24:6; 27:17).

The Normative Guideline

The normative guideline for the church is as follows. The church has a mandate to follow the universal prescriptive passages of the New Testament that relate to how it functions. However, the church is not under obligation to follow the descriptive passages of the New Testament. Scripture is the final authority in these matters!

Questions for Reflection and Discussion

1. Do you believe that churches today should follow the descriptive practices pertaining to the early church? Explain.
2. Should churches today attempt to replicate all or most of the ministry practices of the early church? If so, why? How is this possible? What has this chapter taught you about this view? Explain.
3. Before reading this chapter, were you aware of the city-church and house-church concept? Have can you avoid using eisegesis to interpret passages that refer to these churches?
4. Many argue today that the church is to be led by a plurality of elders. What affect does the city-church and house-church concept have on this view? Is it possible that in the first century, one elder led a house-church?

5. From the information supplied in this chapter, do you believe that you will be able to spot prescriptive passages in their context? Why or why not?
6. This chapter discusses seven universal imperatives. What others would you add to this list?

Endnotes

1. Walter L. Liefeld, *Interpreting the Book of Acts* (Grand Rapids: Baker Book House, 1995), 98.
2. For the sake of argument, I will assume this here and in the material that follows.
3. F. F. Bruce, *Commentary on the Book of Acts* (Grand Rapids: Eerdmans, n.d.), 408.
4. Rex A. Koivisto, *One Lord, One Faith* (Wheaton: Victor, 1993), 27–28. Also, see Robert Banks, *Paul's Idea of Community: The Early House Churches in Their Historical Setting* (Grand Rapids: Eerdmans, 1980); and Abraham J. Malherbe, *Social Aspects of Early Christianity* (Baton Rouge: Louisiana State University Press, 1977), 70.
5. Koivisto, *One Lord, One Faith,* 28.
6. New Testament scholar Gordon D. Fee also suggests that each house-church had its own elder or elders. Gordon D. Fee, *Gospel and Spirit* (Peabody, Mass.: Hendrickson, 1991), 55.
7. Many church practices exist. See my list of twenty such practices in chapter 7.
8. Fee concurs, *Gospel and Spirit,* 94.
9. Alexander Strauch, *Biblical Eldership* (Littleton, Colo.: Lewis & Roth, 1986), 11.
10. Ibid.
11. Fee, *Gospel and Spirit,* 95.
12. I am primarily considering passages in Acts and the epistles of the New Testament.
13. This is the third principle discussed in chapter 4 concerning the interpretation and application of biblical narratives. As we stated there, the author used this material for descriptive and sequential purposes. Though we need this information to fill in the details, it's not as crucial as other data in the book.
14. There are some exceptions to this statement. For instance, there are specific, personal, and local imperatives. I'll cover them below.
15. Daniel B. Wallace, *Greek Grammar Beyond the Basics* (Grand Rapids: Zondervan, 1996), 485.
16. Liefeld, *Interpreting the Book of Acts,* 113.

17. The subjunctive mood is a verb form that represents a denoted act or state, not as a fact, but as a contingent or possibility.
18. Wallace, *Greek Grammar Beyond the Basics,* 464.
19. Ibid., 608.
20. A participle of attendant circumstance.
21. Wallace, *Greek Grammar Beyond the Basics,* 642.
22. This is a participle of attendant circumstance combined with a hortatory subjunctive.
23. Wallace, *Greek Grammar Beyond the Basics,* 650.
24. Ibid., 569.
25. See Exodus 20:17 and Deuteronomy 5:21.
26. See also Walter Grundmann, *dei,* in *Theological Dictionary of the New Testament,* vol. 2 (Grand Rapids: Eerdmans, 1964), 21, 24.
27. Also see Joachim Jeremias, *boulemai,* in *Theological Dictionary of the New Testament*, vol 1 (Grand Rapids: Eerdman's, 1964), 632.
28. In Roman times it was common for writers to place personal remarks and final greetings at the end of their letters.
29. Titus 1:5 is one verse where the appointment of elders was enjoined. The question here is, Was each involved in leading a housechurch in the town?

7

The Hermeneutic of Patterns Versus Principles

Must all churches everywhere always follow the practices as well as the principles of the early church? A congregation could respond with two possible answers. One concerns following both the practices and the patterns of the early church. This is the topic of the first section of this chapter. The other answer considers following only the principles underlying the practices of the early church. This will be the topic of the second section of this chapter. I will conclude by stating a normative principle for the church today.

The Hermeneutic of Patternism

One answer to the opening question posed above is that all congregations everywhere must always follow the practices and patterns of the early church. Supposedly what the apostles had the early church practice represents universal and binding apostolic precepts. This is the hermeneutic of patternism. I will articulate this position, show the evidence in support of this view, provide some examples, and then evaluate it.

The Position

It is argued that God has a purpose for recording in Scripture the practices and patterns of the early church. They serve to help all Christians in the following centuries know how to conduct their church ministries. This information serves as a blueprint, or guide, that we can use to direct our churches today. Consequently, if we desire to replicate the exciting, expansive ministry of the early church, we need to follow its practices. In other words, we need to do ministry in the way they did it.

The Support

I will discuss three proofs that are typically offered in support of the hermeneutic of patternism. First, Christ and His apostles established the New Testament church. They determined its structure, form, and ministries, and they did it as well as one could expect. It's thus presumptuous on our part to assume that we could do it any better today. Hence, we are wise to emulate what they did.

Second, God blessed the early church and its ministries. Many people came to faith in Christ and the congregations grew remarkably. For example, the church in Jerusalem began with three thousand converts (Acts 2:41), and later the number of men alone grew to about five thousand (4:4). If we want God to bless us as He blessed them, then we must do ministry the way they did ministry.

Third, Scripture teaches that congregations today must observe the biblical practices and patterns of the early church. According to such passages as 1 Corinthians 11:16 and 14:37, believers down through the centuries must follow the practices enjoined by the apostles in the early church. Thus, apostolic practice is apostolic precept for all churches.

Some Examples

In chapter 7 we noted several of the practices and patterns of the early church. The following discussion will serve as a quick review. One practice is when the churches met. Some congregations gathered every day (Acts 2:46; 5:42), whereas others met on the first day of the week (Acts 20:7; 1 Cor. 16:2). A second practice is how the congregations met. The early church consisted of city-churches (Acts 2:46; 5:42; 20:20) and house-churches (Acts 2:46; 12:12–17; Rom. 16:3–5; 1 Cor. 16:19).

A third practice is what the churches did when they met. Some were characterized by the following: the apostles' teaching, fellowship, prayer, the breaking of bread, the sharing of possessions, worship, evangelism, the exercise of spiritual gifts (such as speaking in tongues and prophesying), and fasting (Acts 2:42–47; 4:32–36; 1 Cor. 14:26–33). A fourth practice concerns who led the churches. The leaders consisted of the apostles (Acts 6:1–6), the elders (20:17), and occasionally a prominent individual such as James (12:17; 15:13–21; 21:18).

In addition to the preceding, I have listed the following twenty early-church practices (see the discussion connected with problem #4). Some examples worth mentioning here include the casting of lots to select a replacement leader (Acts 1:15–26) and greeting one another with a holy kiss (Rom. 16:16).

The Evaluation

It's important that we carefully evaluate the hermeneutic of patternism. I find no less than nine problems with this view. Let's consider each in turn.

Problem #1

Patternism wrongly assumes that everyone in the early church shared the same practices and patterns. Supposedly these activities are divinely given and thus universally mandated. Regrettably, advocates of this view see the early church as a homogeneous monolith, rather than made up of culturally distinct congregations.

In at least one case, other churches followed the lead of a congregation regarding the way women should pray in a corporate worship service (1 Cor. 11:16). But in many other instances, individual congregations adopted their own unique practices and patterns. For example, the church in Jerusalem met daily (Acts 2:46), whereas the congregation in Troas met on the first day of the week (Acts 20:7). Paul advised the widows in Ephesus to remarry (1 Tim. 5:14), whereas he encouraged those in Corinth to remain single (1 Cor. 7:39–40). The religious leaders at the Jerusalem Council urged Gentile converts to "abstain from eating food sacrificed to idols" (Acts 15:29), but Paul permitted the practice in the church in Corinth (see the discussion in 1 Cor. 8–10).[1]

Some have incorrectly concluded that the local imperative recorded in 1 Corinthians 14:37 is a universal injunction. They fail to note that Paul specifically applied his directive to the church in Corinth ("I am writing to you"). Paul was regulating the practice of speaking in tongues and prophesying, as well as the participation of women in the corporate worship service (see vv. 26–35).

Problem #2

If all congregations everywhere are to follow the practices of the early church, which specific activities are normative? Are believers to follow the practices of the church in Jerusalem, Syrian Antioch, Rome, Corinth, Galatia, Ephesus, Thessalonica, Philippi, or Colosse?

The Bible most likely doesn't record all the practices that were prevalent among the congregations of the first century A.D. Imagine the Holy Spirit allowing a sequel to Acts to be written today. What practices do you think He would permit to be mentioned, and which ones do you think He would allow to be ignored? I suspect that most of our contemporary and traditional church practices, though constructive and good, wouldn't be included in such a work.

Problem #3

We don't have much information on any particular congregation of the first century. This means that many church practices are not mentioned in the Bible. And the ones that are mentioned raise more questions than they answer about the way the early church conducted its ministry.

For example, we know that the Jerusalem church met every day and observed the practices recorded in Acts 2:42–47. However, it's not clear whether this routine continued indefinitely. The church in Troas met on the first day of the week and observed the Lord's Supper then (Acts 20:7). Yet it's not definite whether this pattern was true in every instance. The church in Corinth observed the Lord's Supper and used some of their worship time to exercise spiritual gifts (1 Cor. 11:20–34; 14:26–35). But it's unknown whether this paradigm remained in effect throughout the life of the church.

The hermeneutic of patternism advocates taking all the early church practices recorded in the New Testament and combining them to create a composite picture of how a typical first-century

A.D. congregation operated. However, this approach fails to consider that some practices would conflict (such as meeting every day as opposed to meeting only once a week). Additionally, Scripture nowhere mandates that believers must create a composite picture. In fact, trying to do so would be pointless and frustrating.

Problem #4

If we must follow the practices of the early church, then *all* of them, not just *some* of them, must be imitated. Otherwise, we're just arbitrarily choosing the ones we like and discarding the rest. Truly such an approach would be inconsistent and hypocritical![2] The following is a list of twenty early church practices. If we emulate some of these, then why not all of them?

Early-Church Practices

1. Selecting a leader by casting lots (Acts 1:15–26)
2. Practicing common ownership and the generous distribution of goods (Acts 2:44–45; 4:32)
3. Greeting one another with a holy kiss (Rom. 16:16; 1 Cor. 16:20; 2 Cor. 13:12; 1 Thess. 5:26; 1 Peter 5:14)
4. Abstaining from meats offered to idols (Acts 15:29; 1 Cor. 8:9–13)
5. Women praying with their heads covered (1 Cor. 11:5)
6. Going up to the temple at three in the afternoon (Acts 3:1)
7. Speaking in tongues and prophesying (1 Cor. 14:5)
8. Prohibiting women from speaking in a corporate worship service (1 Cor. 14:34)   *Speaking in tongues from the context*
9. Abstaining from eating blood and the meat of strangled animals (Acts 15:28–29)
10. Baptizing for the dead (1 Cor. 15:29)
11. Anointing the sick with olive oil and praying for their healing (James 5:14–15)
12. Preaching in synagogues on the Sabbath (Acts 14:1; 17:2–3)
13. Lifting up holy hands while praying (1 Tim. 2:8)
14. Supporting widows over the age of sixty (1 Tim. 5:9)
15. Taking collections in the church for the poor (1 Cor. 16:1)

16. Meeting in homes (Acts 2:46–47; Rom. 16:3–5, 14–15; 1 Cor. 16:19)
17. Leading by means of elders (Acts 11:30; 14:23; 15; 20:17; James 5:14–15)
18. Gathering every day (Acts 2:46), and especially on the first day of the week (Acts 20:7; 1 Cor. 16:2)
19. Sending and receiving of missionaries (Acts 13:1–3; 14:26–28)
20. Drinking wine, in addition to water (1 Tim. 5:23)

Problem #5

Just because the early church followed certain practices doesn't mean that believers today are mandated to do the same.[3] If the reasoning of the hermeneutic of patternism is analyzed, we discover a *non sequitur* argument, namely, one in which the conclusion doesn't follow from the evidence. There must first be a command, that is, a universal imperative.[4] In the absence of this, the practice is not binding on churches today.

Proponents of the hermeneutic of patternism maintain that churches down through the centuries have remained similar in many ways. And despite the passage of almost two millennia, the goals and needs of the church are strikingly alike. Therefore, the practices and patterns evident in the early church allegedly should also be present in churches today.

But this line of reasoning rests on a false analogy. Despite some resemblances, there are also vast differences between the early church and the modern church. These distinctions can't be ignored just because of the similarities. Likewise, the presence of similarities doesn't prove that practices and patterns in the first-century church are binding today. As the French proverb says, "To compare is not to prove."[5]

Problem #6

We must determine whether an author's intent for discussing a specific early church practice was to establish a precedent. For example, did Luke include Acts 2:26 to teach us that church leaders need to be chosen by casting lots? Obviously not! Did he include verse 46 to mandate that believers needed to meet together every day? The answer is *no*. Both of these practices (as well as many others) are incidental to the author's purpose and weren't intended to be normative.

Problem #7

As we discovered in chapter 6, many of the passages concerning early church practices are descriptive in nature and thus not binding on congregations today. The author was simply reporting what took place, not mandating an unchanging practice.

Problem #8

Patternism can easily lead to three serious problems for the church. The first is the mistaken conclusion that those who don't agree that a certain early-church practice is binding are unbiblical and disobedient to God. Supposedly they're not conducting their ministries in the way that God wants.

The second problem is that the hermeneutic of patternism can lead to a judgmental attitude toward others.[6] For example, I know of a popular Bible teacher who castigates a large North American church for holding a service for seekers on the first day of the week. This person maintains this critical attitude despite the clear teaching of Romans 14:5–8, which permits such a service!

The third problem is that the hermeneutic of patternism can delude us into thinking that we have a corner market on the truth. We convince ourselves that we have "superior" knowledge. This in turn causes us to become inflated with pride. Scripture rightly condemns such arrogance.[7]

Problem #9

The hermeneutic of patternism fails to consider the dynamic nature of the church. Liefeld writes, "So Acts describes a changing pattern of leadership and authority due to the nature of the church as 'emerging' rather than static."[8] The apostles were still on the scene and heavily involved in most of its practices. However, today's church is nonapostolic—the apostles are no longer present. The church's situation has changed sufficiently that various apostolic practices (many of which are listed on pages 90-91) don't fit today's nonapostolic churches.

In light of this discussion, what should be our response to the practices and patterns of ministry evident in the early church? First, we need to recognize that incidental actions occurring among first-century believers aren't mandates to be followed for the rest of time. Second, we are free to choose what to observe and what not to observe. Third, we should consider whether there is a biblical principle behind an early church practice. If so, we may want to think about how we can apply that principle in a contemporary way.

Let's consider an example. In some cases, believers met every day (Acts 2:46). On other occasions they gathered together on the first day of the week (1 Cor. 16:2). The timeless principle is that the church met for corporate worship (Heb. 10:25). A congregation of believers is free to decide when and where to meet. However, they must not judge others who choose to meet under different circumstances and at other times (Rom. 14:5–13).

A Summary Evaluation of Patternism

1. Patternism wrongly assumes that all the churches shared the same practices and patterns.
2. If all congregations everywhere are to follow the practices of the early church, which church's specific activities are normative?
3. We have only a small amount of information about the practices of the early church. How do we fill in the gaps to obtain a complete picture?
4. If we must follow the practices of the early church, then *all* of them, not just *some* of them, must be imitated.
5. Just because the early church followed certain practices doesn't mean that believers today are mandated to do the same.

6. We must determine whether an author's intent for discussing a specific early church practice was to establish a precedent.
7. Many of the passages concerning early church practices are descriptive in nature and thus not binding on congregations today.
8. Patternism can lead to a condemning, judgmental, and arrogant attitude.
9. The church is dynamic and has changed sufficiently that many apostolic practices no longer fit today's nonapostolic churches.

More Support

Numerous advocates of patternism argue that some practices of the early church were merely cultural and thus not normative for congregations today. Supposedly believers should emulate only those ministry patterns that are based on biblical principles. For instance, the early church met in homes because it was convenient and necessary during times of persecution. However, this practice allegedly is not supported by any biblical principle and thus is not necessary to be observed by churches today.

This train of thought is flawed for two reasons. First, those making such an argument fail to understand that all church practices (not just some) are influenced by culture. In fact, neither individual believers nor the congregations to which they belong can separate themselves from their culture. Thus, it's fallacious to make the presence or absence of culture the determining factor when evaluating the continuing applicability of ministry patterns within the early church.

Second, behind most practices of the first-century church is a general principle worth considering. For example, the early church met in homes. We don't discount this practice just because it was influenced by cultural forces. Rather, the determining factor is the nature and applicability of the timeless principle behind the ministry pattern. In this case, the idea is that believers should regularly gather together for corporate worship (Heb. 10:25).

From this example we see that the enduring principles, not the specific practices, are most important to consider and emulate. That the church meets regularly (the principle) is far more consequential than where or when it meets (the ministry patterns).

The Hermeneutic of Principalism

We have examined patternism and found it objectionable. Now let's turn our attention to the hermeneutic of principalism. We'll discover that the church is obligated to follow the principles, but not necessarily the ministry practices and patterns, of the early church.

The Position

As noted earlier, we're not obligated to follow the practices of the early church. Nevertheless, we should know and apply the principles that characterize all churches, regardless of whether the congregations are ancient or contemporary. Applying biblical principles implies that we agree with what Scripture teaches, we allow God's Word to transform our thinking, and we let the truth influence the way we operate our church ministries.

This view is based on the premise that the principles of Scripture are normative for all churches everywhere. They are stated in propositional form and reflect the theological truth of Scripture, especially as it pertains to the church. These assertions are not framed as commands or imperatives, but rather as statements of being. Here's an example: the church *is* the body of Christ.

While biblical principles related to the church aren't couched as imperatives, they are nonetheless worthy of being embraced and applied. In other words, truths about the nature of the church should affect how it conducts its ministries. For example, the church exists (in part) to reach the lost for Christ. This propositional statement should prompt the church to get involved in evangelistic activities. Here's another example. The ordinances of baptism and the Lord's Supper are an integral part of the church. This theological truth should lead to the regular observance of these rites among believers.

Imagine collecting and organizing all this information about principles for doing ministry. The result would be a theology of the church, or ecclesiology. While the practices of congregations change and are nonbinding, the propositional truths about the church remain the same. Because they transcend history and culture, they are normative and binding on all churches down through the centuries. √

Some Examples

The following are some examples of ecclesiological principles that believers throughout church history should observe.

- The church's beliefs are based on Scripture (2 Tim. 3:16–17).
- The church's purpose is to glorify God (Rom. 15:6; 1 Cor. 6:20; 10:31).
- The church's mission is to make disciples (Matt. 28:19–20; Mark 16:15).
- The church is the body of Christ universal and local (Matt. 16:16–19; Acts 9:31; Gal. 1:13; Eph. 1:22–23; Col. 1:18).
- The church is to meet together regularly (Heb. 10:25).
- The church is to celebrate the ordinances (Matt. 26:26–29; 28:19; Acts 2:38; 1 Cor. 11:23–26).
- The church is to discipline its people (Matt. 18:15–17;1 Cor. 5:1–5).
- The church is to teach Scripture (2 Tim. 4:2).
- The church is to evangelize the lost (Matt. 28:19–20).
- The church is to obey its leaders (Heb. 13:17).
- The church is to pay its workers (1 Cor. 9:14; 1 Tim. 5:18).

The Normative Guideline

God wants Christians to believe and observe the principles about church ministry taught in Scripture, for they are normative. In contrast, believers aren't obligated to follow early-church practices and patterns of ministry.

Questions for Reflection and Discussion

1. It's natural for churches to want to follow early-church practices and patterns. What first-century practices does your church follow? Why? Is this okay? Shouldn't other churches follow them as well? Explain.
2. What are the best arguments for patternism? Explain. What are the best arguments against patternism? Explain.
3. What would happen in your church if it followed the hermeneutic of principalism? Would there be few or many changes?
4. How would you deal with people who held to the hermeneutic of patternism, especially those who criticize your church and its ministry? For example, what would you say to them?
5. How has this chapter helped you to think about the ministry of your church?

Endnotes

1. Some would view these examples as contradictions and, thus, would work hard at reconciling the texts. However, a simpler approach is that these churches exercised their freedom to treat their circumstances differently.
2. Fee and Stuart agree. See Gordon D. Fee and Douglas Stuart, *How to Read the Bible for All It's Worth* (Grand Rapids: Zondervan, 1981), 71.
3. The exception is when Scripture makes it clear that we're to follow a specific practice (i.e., observing the Lord's Supper).
4. This is an injunction that is normative for today. In contrast, local imperatives are normative only at the time they were written.
5. A. J. Hoover, *Don't You Believe It!* (Chicago: Moody, 1982), 49.
6. Note that Paul strongly condemns this in Romans 14:10–13.
7. In 1 Corinthians 8:1–2, Paul said that while knowledge may make us feel important, it is love that really builds up the church. Likewise, anyone who claims to know all the answers doesn't really know very much.
8. Walter L. Liefeld, *Interpreting the Book of Acts* (Grand Rapids: Baker, 1995), 97–98.

8

The Hermeneutic of
Functions Versus Forms

In *The E-Myth*, Michael Gerber writes: "Today's world is a difficult place. Mankind has experienced more change in the past twenty years than in the 2,000 that preceded them."[1] The result is accelerating, chaotic times. Regardless of the instability of our age, Christ has commissioned the church to minister in His name to the lost. Undoubtedly, believers could benefit from a well-written theology of change.

What's the role of change in conducting the ministries of the church? What can and can't we change? Here's a stronger way of asking this question: What must we change, and what must we never change? The answer that a church gives reflects its theology of change. Most congregations respond in either one of two ways. The first section of this chapter presents the first answer, namely, the hermeneutic of forms. The second section provides the second answer, namely, the hermeneutic of functions. I then conclude with a normative statement for the church.

The Hermeneutic of Forms

A helpful way to view change in the local church and its ministries is to examine its functions and forms. The key question to ask is this: What can the church change, and what shouldn't it change? One answer is that the church's forms as well as its functions must not change appreciably. This view is what I refer to as the hermeneutic

101

of forms. In this section, I will define functions and forms and then distinguish between them. Then I will present the position and provide several examples of the hermeneutic of forms.

The Definitions

Functions

The church's functions are what it's supposed to accomplish. They are biblical mandates that answer the *what* question, namely, *what* are we supposed to be doing? The functions consist of the church's required activities (such as evangelism, worship, fellowship, community outreach, biblical instruction and proclamation, leadership training, organizational development, observance of the ordinances, and discipleship, as well as others).

Each function has meaning. The following are some examples. Communion is a remembrance of Christ's death. Evangelism is telling people how to have a relationship with Christ. Prayer is talking with God. Baptism is being identified with Christ's death and resurrection. Teaching is the communication of God's truth. And organization is guiding the church to function in a fitting and orderly way.

The Meaning of Functions	
Function	*Meaning*
1. Communion	Remembering Christ's death
2. Evangelism	Telling people how to have a relationship with Christ
3. Prayer	Talking with God
4. Baptism	Being identified with Christ's death and resurrection
5. Teaching	Communicating God's truth
6. Organization	Guiding the church to function in a fitting and orderly way

You can discover a church's functions by asking whether a particular activity of a congregation is an end or a means to an end.

<u>Functions are ends in themselves.</u> You first need to discover the so-called function's meaning. Then you should ask whether this is an end or a means to an end.[2]

Forms

The forms are how the church accomplishes what it does, namely, its functions or activities. Forms serve the functions. They answer the *how* question, that is, *how* will the church accomplish its functions? The forms consist of the church's methods for ministry. The methods would include an activity such as the mode of baptism (whether immersion, sprinkling, or pouring). It would also include the church's style of worship (whether traditional or contemporary), and its style of evangelism (whether relational or confrontational).

Forms not only accomplish the functions but also help convey the meanings of those functions. For example, the meaning of the Lord's Supper is that it's a remembrance of Christ's death. In 1 Corinthians 11:26, Paul stated that the observance of this rite is a proclamation of Christ's death. Another example is baptism. The observance of this ordinance reminds believers of their identification with Christ's death and resurrection (Rom. 6:3–4).

Culture often dictates the particular forms that the church uses (1 Chron. 12:32). For example, not many people respond any longer to a city-wide crusade unless it's one of Billy Graham's popular campaigns. However, they may respond to an invitation to an informal home Bible study where someone presents the gospel. We can insist on using the crusade approach, but we should not be surprised when few show up.

You can discover a ministry's form by asking whether the form or model in question is an end or a means to an end. <u>Forms are means to ends.</u> For example, do we conduct small groups simply for the sake of having these types of meetings, or do they serve a greater purpose?[3]

The Position

Now that we know what functions and forms are, we're ready to examine the hermeneutic of form. There are two views concerning this worth mentioning.

One is that the functions shouldn't change, and neither should those forms that are early-church practices. This is a teaching of patternism (a concept that we covered in chapter 7). Not all forms are absolute, only those that are early-church practices that reflect apostolic precepts. We may change any other forms but not those that are supposedly apostolic in nature. The support for this view and its evaluation are the same as those for patternism (which we discussed in chapter 7).

The other view is that the functions and forms shouldn't change regardless of whether they reflect early-church practices or apostolic precepts. Little proof is offered in support for this view. It's an opinion generally held by well-meaning people who are tradition-bound and fear change. The critique of this view is the same as that found in chapter 1 on tradition.

Some Examples

Several examples of the hermeneutic of form exist in today's churches. Each function includes a specific, nonchanging form. For example, some would argue that the correct form for the function of communion is wine and unleavened bread. The correct form for the function of leadership is elder rule. The only legitimate form for the function of baptism is immersion. The correct form for the function of worship is the great hymns of the faith accompanied by a pipe organ and piano. Finally, a growing number of churches believe that the correct form for the function of worship is the more contemporary American format, which consists of up-to-date music that is accompanied by drums, guitars, and similar types of instuments.

Some Examples of the Hermeneutic Form	
Function	*Form*
1. Communion	Wine and unleavened bread
2. Leadership	Elder rule
3. Baptism	Immersion
4. Worship	Traditional

The Hermeneutic of Functions

This chapter has posed the following question about how the church conducts its ministries: What should change and what should never change? One answer is that the church's forms as well as its functions should not change appreciably. A better answer, however, is that the church is free to change its ministry forms but not its functions. This is what I refer to as the hermeneutic of functions.

The Position

The position of the hermeneutic of functions can be summed up in two principles.

Principle #1

The church has the freedom to make changes in its forms of ministry or how it conducts its ministries. God gives all churches freedom under the guidance of the Holy Spirit to choose the forms or methods that best accomplish their functions (such as evangelism, worship, and so on). These forms are nonmandated and therefore nonabsolutes. This means that each congregation has vast freedom regarding how it implements the functions and ultimately how it conducts its ministries. Simply because the New Testament doesn't mandate or even mention some forms doesn't mean that they are unbiblical or wrong. Rather, it simply means that God has given believers freedom in those areas.

There is a problem and limitation, however, to that freedom. Christians often assume that only one correct interpretation of a concept exists (such as church government or polity). When some biblical texts seem to differ with one another, we should first attempt to reconcile those texts. For example, when we encounter the different views of church government (namely, Episcopalian, Presbyterian, and Congregational), we assume that only one of these is the correct option and begin to look for Scripture passages to validate it.

It's always good to check what we believe about church government with the teaching of Scripture. But what if after investigating the biblical evidence, we find that we can't entirely reconcile our view with God's Word? We must then be open to the idea that more than one view of church government is supported in Scripture and that these options don't necessarily contradict one another.

By way of example, consider Paul's instructions to widows. In 1 Corinthians 7:8 he advised them not to marry, but in 1 Timothy 5:14 he counseled some to remarry. The apostle was not contradicting himself; rather, he was dealing with different situations that called for different responses. In the same way, the preceding three forms of church government have scriptural support. Believers have the freedom to use the form that best serves the church's functions according to its current situation.

I only suggest two restrictions that we should consider in exercising our freedom to choose forms. The first is that the forms must agree with the Bible. This means that while the forms may not be found in Scripture, they must not contradict or disagree in any way with the teaching of God's Word.[4] Why? Because Scripture is the final authority. It sets the boundaries, and each local church is free under the guidance of the Holy Spirit to minister within those boundaries.

The second restriction is that we must be careful in the context of exercising our freedom not to judge or condemn those who choose to place themselves under obligations, such as worshiping on the first day of the week and serving the Lord's Supper weekly. Similarly, those who in their freedom choose to observe certain early-church practices must not criticize or mandate for other congregations who decide to do otherwise. Paul sternly warned against any display of a legalistic attitude (Rom. 14:5–12).

I want to issue a warning. Our forms—whatever the function—help us to accomplish biblical absolutes that best serve Christ.[5] The note of caution is to avoid getting locked into a particular form, which, in turn, causes you to refuse to change how you conduct your church ministry. When a form ceases to be effective, it is imperative that we exercise our freedom and look for and embrace other more workable forms that minister better to people.

Francis Schaeffer warned, "Not being able, as times change, to change under the Holy Spirit is ugly. The same applies to church polity and practice. In a rapidly changing age like ours, an age of total upheaval like ours, to make nonabsolutes absolutes guarantees both isolation and the death of the institutional, organized church."[6]

Principle #2

The first principle teaches that the church has freedom to change its ministry forms. The second says that when exercising this freedom, the church must never change its functions. Of course, the church may change and in most cases must change its forms over the years so that it's able to communicate intelligently within its culture to its constituency.[7]

The functions of the church are its timeless, unchanging activities. These are biblically mandated activities that all congregations must pursue in order to fulfill their God-given purpose, namely, to bring glory to the Lord. In contrast, the forms of the church are its temporal, changing practices or methods. Because these are culturally bound, all churches are free to choose whatever forms are appropriate to accomplish their functions. This is the basis for the church's theology of change. The following chart summarizes this theology with its concepts and their distinctions.

A Theology of Change	
Functions	*Forms*
1. Timeless, unchanging (absolutes)	Temporal, changing (non-absolutes)
2. Based on Scripture	Based on culture
3. Mandates (ministry precepts)	Methods (ministry practices)
4. All churches must pursue (found in the Bible)	All churches are free to choose (agrees with the Bible)
5. Accomplishes the church's purpose	Accomplishes the church's functions

Some Examples

Now that we have a proper understanding of the concepts of function and form, its time to consider some examples. The following sections look at functions and forms and how they affect the church's ordinances, worship, and government.

The Church's Ordinances

The first example is the ordinances of the church. Scripture mandates two ordinances: baptism (Matt. 28:20; Acts 2:38) and the Lord's Supper (1 Cor. 11:23–25). While immersion is the form that best represents the meaning of baptism, the church is free to choose immersion, sprinkling, or pouring. This makes sense because it's possible that someone may be in a situation where immersion is impossible.[8]

The church is also free to choose the forms that best convey the meaning of the Lord's Supper. The Communion elements could be crackers, bread, unleavened bread, wine, grape juice, and so on. The cultural backdrop of the church would exert a strong effect on this decision. The church should ask, "What in the culture may best symbolize and communicate the meaning of the function of Communion to the people involved in its service?"[9]

How far can we take the "so on."

Ordinances of the Church	
Functions	*Forms*
1. Baptism (Matt. 28:20)	Immersion, sprinkling, and pouring
2. Communion (1 Cor. 11:23–25)	Crackers, bread, wine, grape juice, and so on

The Church's Worship

The second example is the church's worship. Scripture mandates worship (Eph. 5:19–20). However, we are free to choose the forms that our worship takes and, over time, even change those forms. The two forms, or styles, of worship are traditional and

Blended?

contemporary. These terms are fluid because today's traditional worship was yesterday's contemporary worship, and today's contemporary worship is tomorrow's traditional worship.

In the past few centuries up until the present day, much of the traditional worship and its music in North America originated in Europe. Having come from there, it reflects the European church's traditions, especially those of the Reformation (for example, the hymns and instruments of worship, such as the pipe organ). However, beginning in the 1960s, much of the contemporary worship and music in North America reflects what has originated in the United States. The question is this: Which form accomplishes best the function of worship and ministers to those whom we serve?

Worship	
Function	*Form*
Worship (Eph. 5:19–20)	Traditional or contemporary

The Church's Government

The third example is the church's government. An important aspect of a congregation's organization is its polity, or the way it superintends itself. While Scripture mandates that the church be run in an organized manner (1 Cor. 14:33, 40; Col. 2:5), believers are free to choose the form of government that best fits their congregation's circumstances, whether newly established or older. The options for church government are Congregational (Acts 6:1–6), Episcopal (15:13–21), Presbyterian (1 Tim. 5:17), or a variation thereof.

Different church groups opt for a different form of government based on their understanding of the Bible. This reflects their effort to reconcile the different passages of Scripture on this topic. While it's possible that God's Word recognizes only one form of church government, it's more likely that differing forms are reflected in Scripture and thus are legitimate.

Church Government	
Function	*Form*
Church government	Congregational, Episcopal,
(1 Cor. 14:33, 40; Col. 2:5)	and Presbyterian

The Normative Guideline

God has given churches today as well as in the first century much freedom as to the forms they can take for their ministries. They are free to choose those forms that best implement their functions. However, they don't have this same liberty with their functions. They must actively pursue the balanced implementation of all the New Testament ecclesiastical functions.

Questions for Reflection and Discussion

1. As you examine your views toward the ministries and practices of your church, have you followed a form or function hermeneutic? Explain.
2. What functions does your church observe? What vital functions of the church seem to be missing? Why? What will you do about this?
3. How willing are you to change the forms that the ministries of your church take? How willing is the church board? The members of the church? Will this be easy or hard? Why?
4. Why should you be willing to change your ministry forms? Will you? Why or why not?
5. Do you have a theology of change? In what ways has this chapter helped you to develop a theology of change?

Endnotes

1. Michael E. Gerber, *The E-Myth* (New York: Harper Brothers, 1986), 156.
2. Actually functions have an end as well. They all work together to accomplish the church's purpose, which is to glorify God (Rom. 15:6; 1 Cor. 6:20).
3. Here's a note for clarification. First, the church's functions and forms aren't to be confused with its principles. (The latter was discussed

in the previous chapter.) Whereas the functions ask the *what* and *how* questions, the principles ask the *why* question. Second, in chapter 5, I covered the prescriptive versus the descriptive hermeneutic. Prescriptive and descriptive passages also affect form and function. For example, prescriptive passages help to identify the church's functions, whereas descriptive passages provide examples of first-century forms.

4. This is similar to the idea in 1 Corinthians 9:21, where Paul said that when he was around people who were without the Law (namely, Gentiles), he became like one not having the Law. And this was permissible. Nevertheless, he abided by the law of Christ.

5. Be it worshiping, teaching, evangelizing, and so on.

6. Francis A. Schaeffer, *The Church at the End of the Twentieth Century* (Wheaton: Crossway, 1970), 68.

7. In an attempt to deal with change, the mainline liberal churches chose to abandon Scripture as an absolute base of authority. They thus recognize many functions. In contrast, numerous other churches (some of them being evangelical congregations) have refused to change their forms, clinging instead to the so-called "tried and true." In both instances, these churches are experiencing steep decline in membership.

8. Also, I don't believe that the New Testament prescribes or dictates any forms of baptism.

9. Some might argue that theology is connected with and conveyed by these original forms. Thus, we shouldn't change them appreciably. It's true that theology may be connected with an original form. However, that's why we change them in different cultures—in other words, to make sure that they convey their proper meaning within the context of that culture.

Aubrey Malphurs is the president of *Vision Ministries International* and is available for consultation and training on various topics related to leadership, values, mission, vision, strategy, church planting, church renewal, and so on. Those wishing to contact him for training, consulting, or speaking engagements may do so through the following:

Vision Ministries International
3909 Swiss Avenue
Dallas, TX 75204
Phone: 214-841-3777
Website: www.visionministry.com